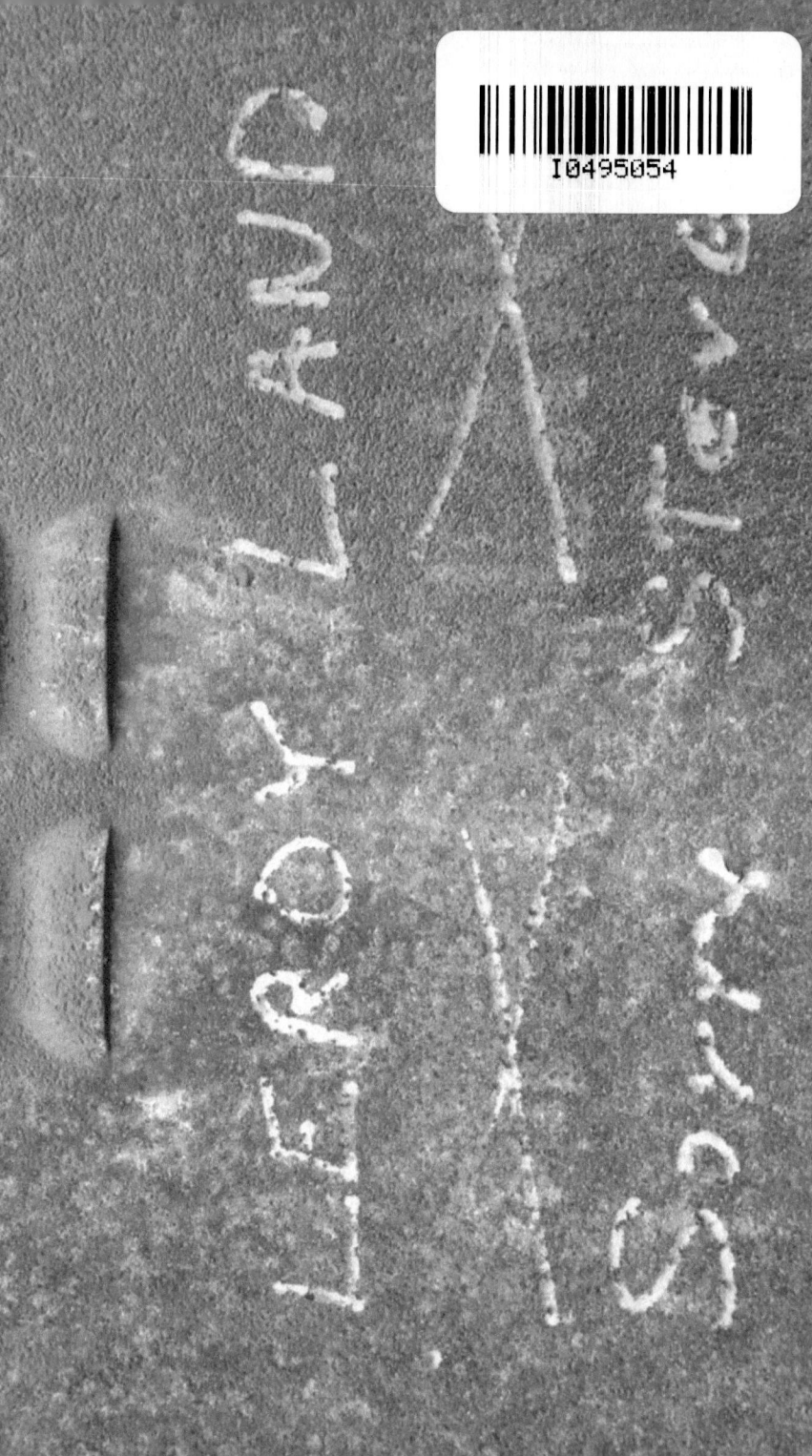

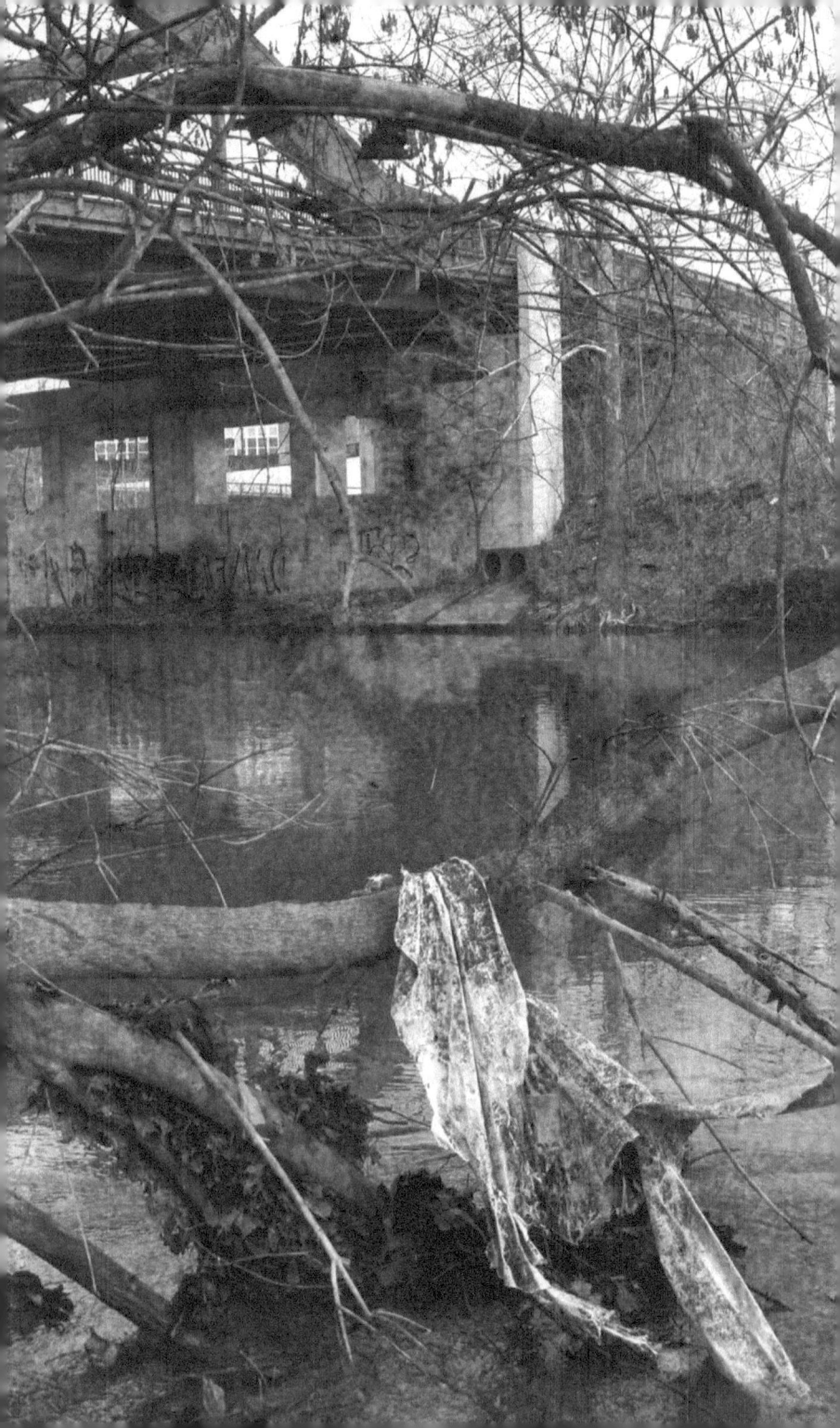

Also by Christopher Lesko

THE GRLZ LIKE VODKA

LONG LIVE CRAZY

THAT'S MY GHOUL

THE ELECTRIC LUNATIC

FUKCED UP

ROXY

DON'T THOWE AWAY PLEASE

SPIDERS ARE LAYING EGGS IN THE LIVING ROOM

VICTIM 666

THE LOCALS ARE WATCHING YOU

Available as ebook and paperback
www.amazon.com/author/leskocrazy

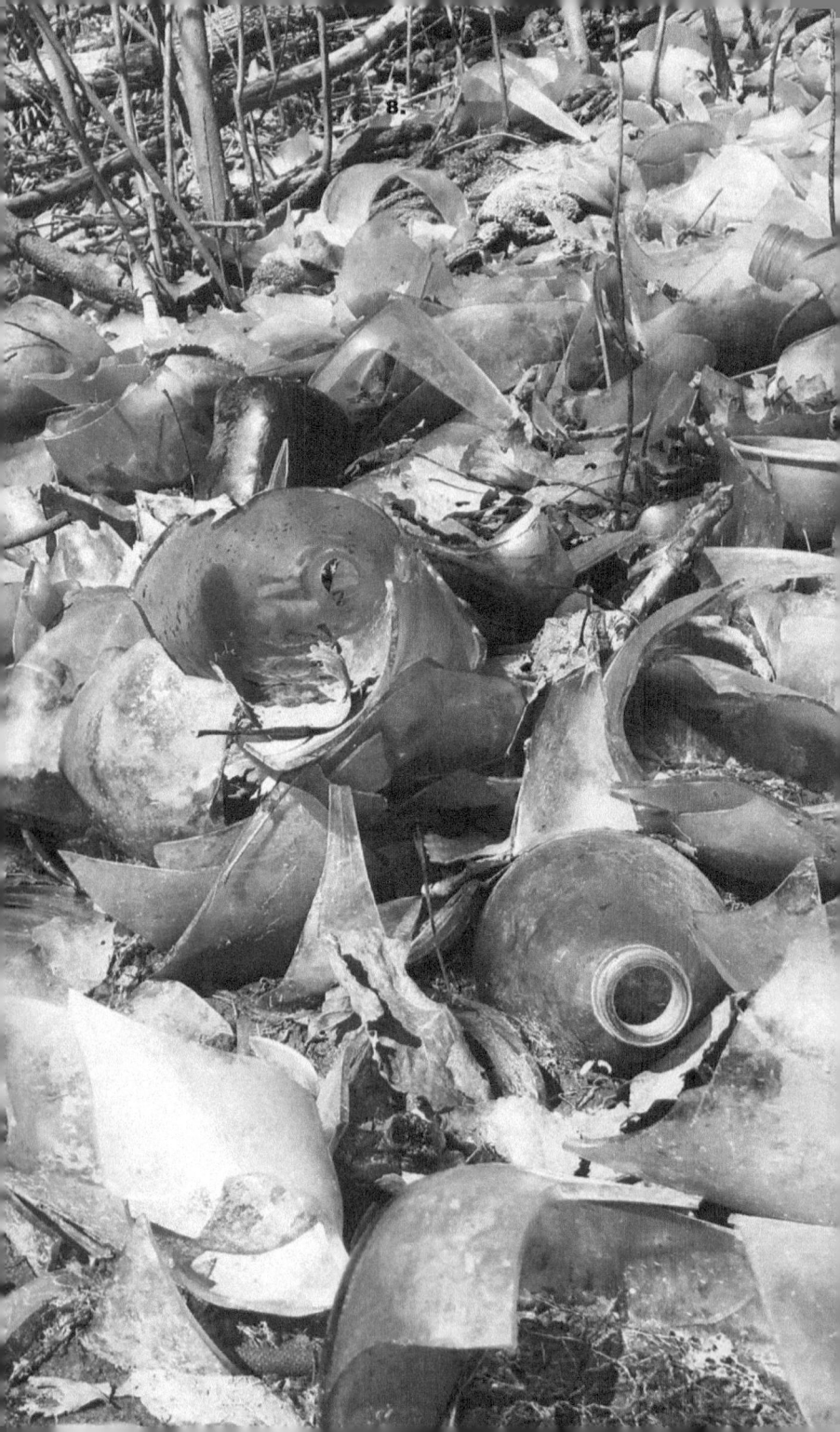

LEROY LAND

(poems & photography)

Christopher Lesko

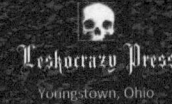

Leskocrazy Press
Youngstown, Ohio

LEROY LAND
Copyright © 2021 Christopher Lesko
Leskocrazy Press
www.amazon.com/author/leskocrazy

ISBN 13: 9798589432060

This is a work of fiction. Names, characters, places, and incidents either are the products of the author's imagination or are used fictitiously. Any resemblance to actual events, locales, or persons, living or dead, is entirely coincidental.

All rights reserved. No part of this book may be reproduced, stored in a retrieval system, or transmitted by any means without the written permission of the author or publisher.

Cover design: Christopher Lesko

My sweet Jenny I'm sinkin' down
Here darlin', in Youngstown

-*Bruce Springsteen*
"Youngstown"

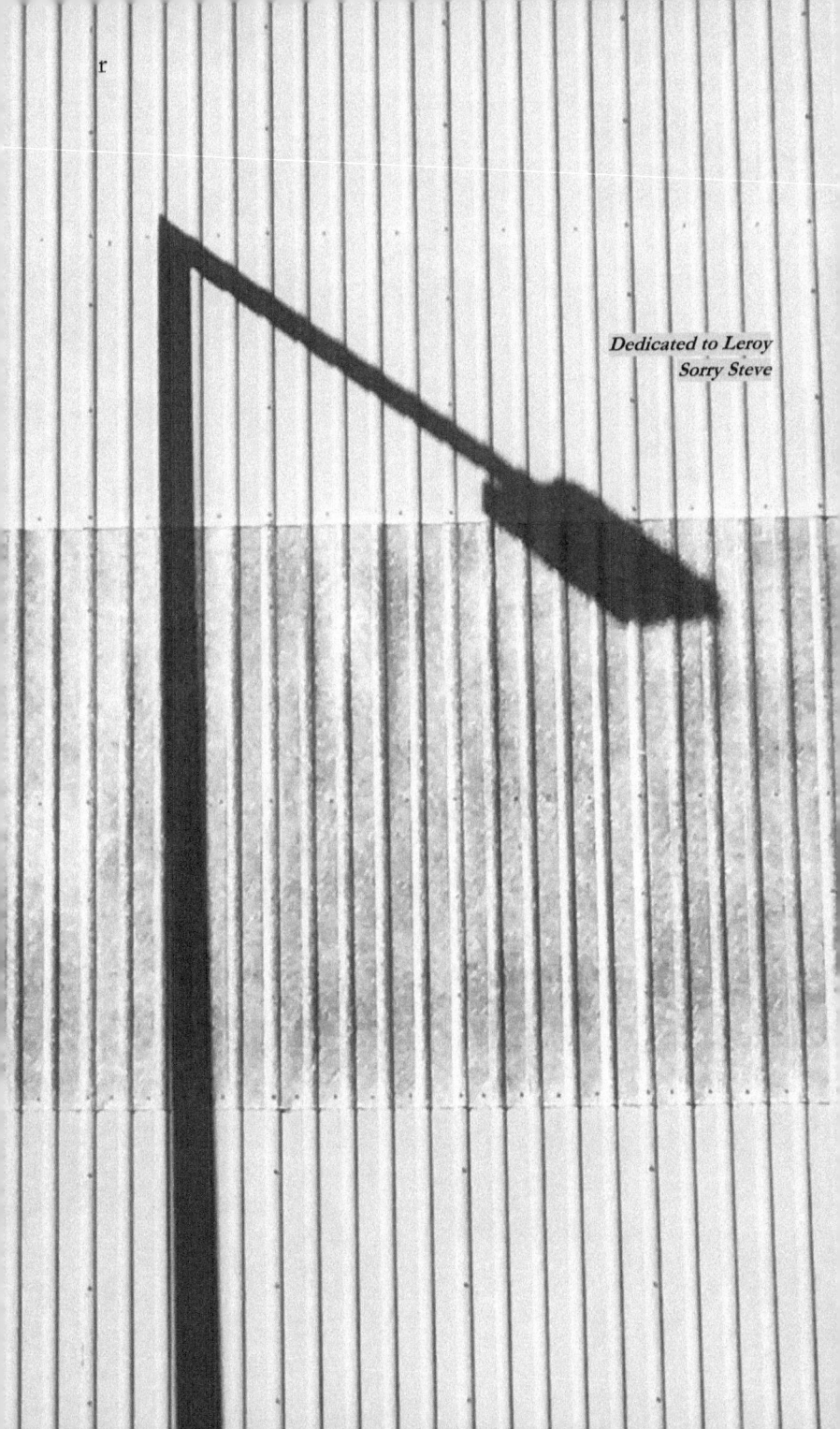

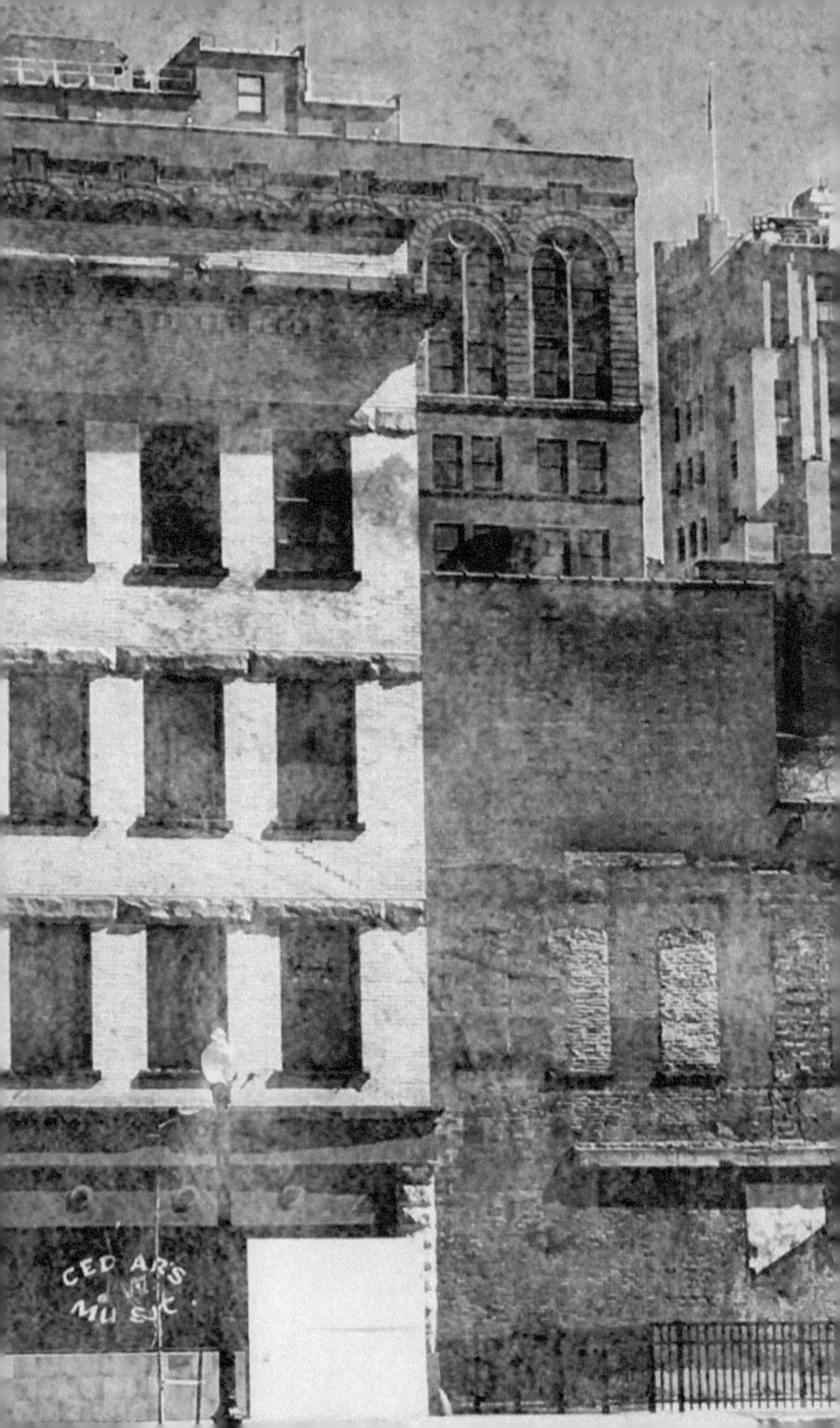

LEROY LAND
><><
Sorry Steve

Leroy AM,
Therefore
He be

LEROY LAND: AN INTRODUCTION

I went on an urban safari to explore abandoned steel mills bleeding rust, leveled warehouses turned to gravel, and the ghost-quiet railroad alongside a burbling river filled with human garbage. Under a large oak tree dead from AIDS, I discovered a withering gray and blue tent with a pathway to it cut through browning wintertime bramble. It appeared to be unoccupied. But it was giving me creepy bad vibes, so I turned around and left.

Something about the tent kept twitching in the back of my mind and a few weeks later I took a friend with me to brave a revisit. "Greetings, my name is Tully, and I come in peace!" I announced to whoever might be inside, cautiously stepping closer to the zipped-up tent. I received no answer. A little gold pad lock on the zipper prevented me from opening the "front door." I understood no one was home. However, lifting a shielding flap to peek through a screen window, I saw something. Yet I told my friend I didn't see anything, not to disturb the sleeping homeless spray paint face inside. "Who was keeping him locked in there? What would happen if I busted off the lock and let him out?" I asked myself as we headed home.

Later that night I went back. Alone. I found the tent unlocked. And guess what? The guy inside was awake! His name is Leroy. He passed me a cold tall boy and had a nice warm camp fire going. So we did shit like cooked and ate chicken pot pies with our bare hands, smoked cigarettes, and burned the cheap-ass earbuds I got from Dollar Tree that broke after one day. One beer led to another and another and after losing count I had him spray paint my face gold like his. That's when magic happened. Leroy began preaching the most poetic words of crazy I'd ever heard. I don't remember leaving that night but woke up piss-soaked behind a dumpster downtown wrapped in a plastic shower curtain. Luckily, I still had all my organs. Unluckily, I had a sickening hangover and had to walk facing the brisk wind for about a mile back to my car while praying it hadn't been towed. But before driving away, I wanted to see Leroy again and laugh with him about how wasted we got.

My mysterious new buddy had vanished. Pathway gone. Tent gone. No muddy footprints in the snow. Not even a pile of ashes or wad of wet toilet paper left behind. Although, if you walk south along the railroad tracks, you'll find written on a rusty electrical box his golden message:

Leroy AM,
Therefore
He be

FREE FOOD

Don't care what they say
Planned Parenthood clinics
always have
the best
ketchup-coated chicky nuggets
in their trash.
Fight me.

CLUB AWESOME

Wasted on illegal toilet wine;
party streamers poppin' out of all my glory holes;
watch my black & blue beaten butt cheeks
jiggle while I twerk:
cage dancing for PIGS
like the ma-cho ma-cho
whatever thing I be.
Oh, fuck yeah,
gimme gimme gimme more
of your
taser.

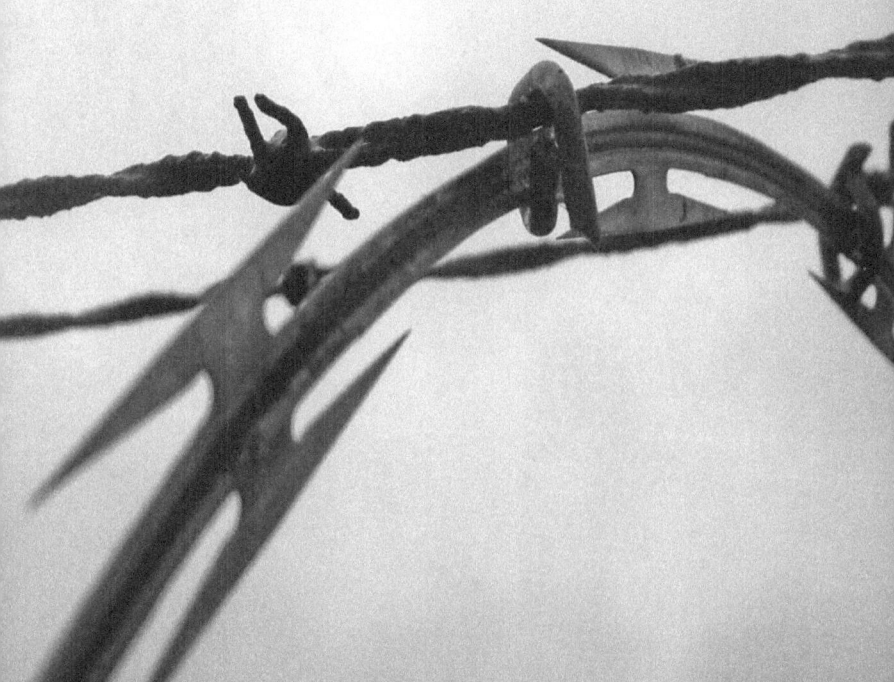

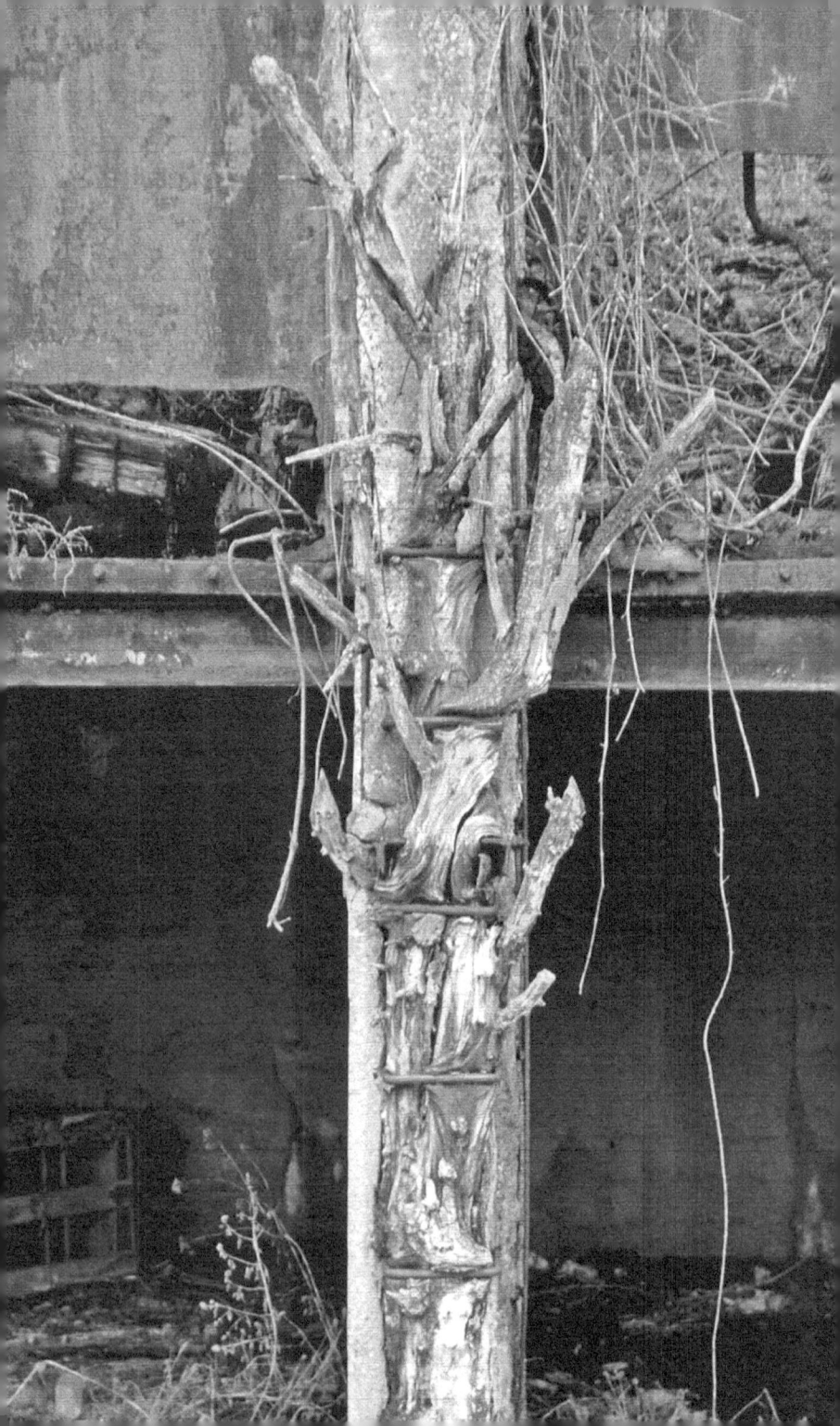

HEY, LEMME BORROW YOUR iPHONE FOR A SEC

Hey, Siri …
Play me the movie *E.T. the Vagina*.

Hey, Siri …
Why does my palm look like there's an egg beneath the skin?

Hey, Siri …
 Do aliens lay eggs?

Hey, Siri …
Am I a human?

Hey, Siri …
Why can't you really say if I'm a human?

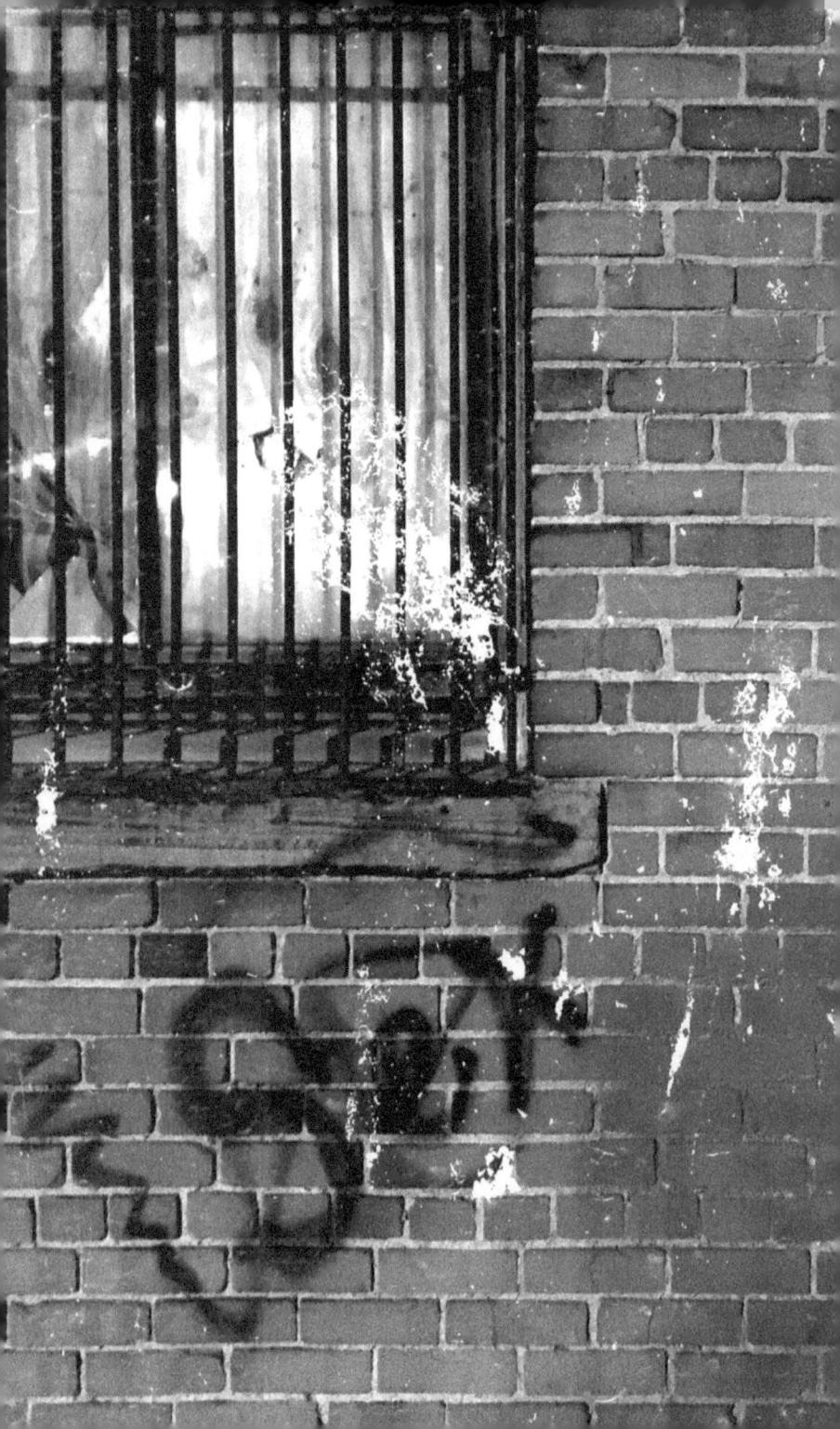

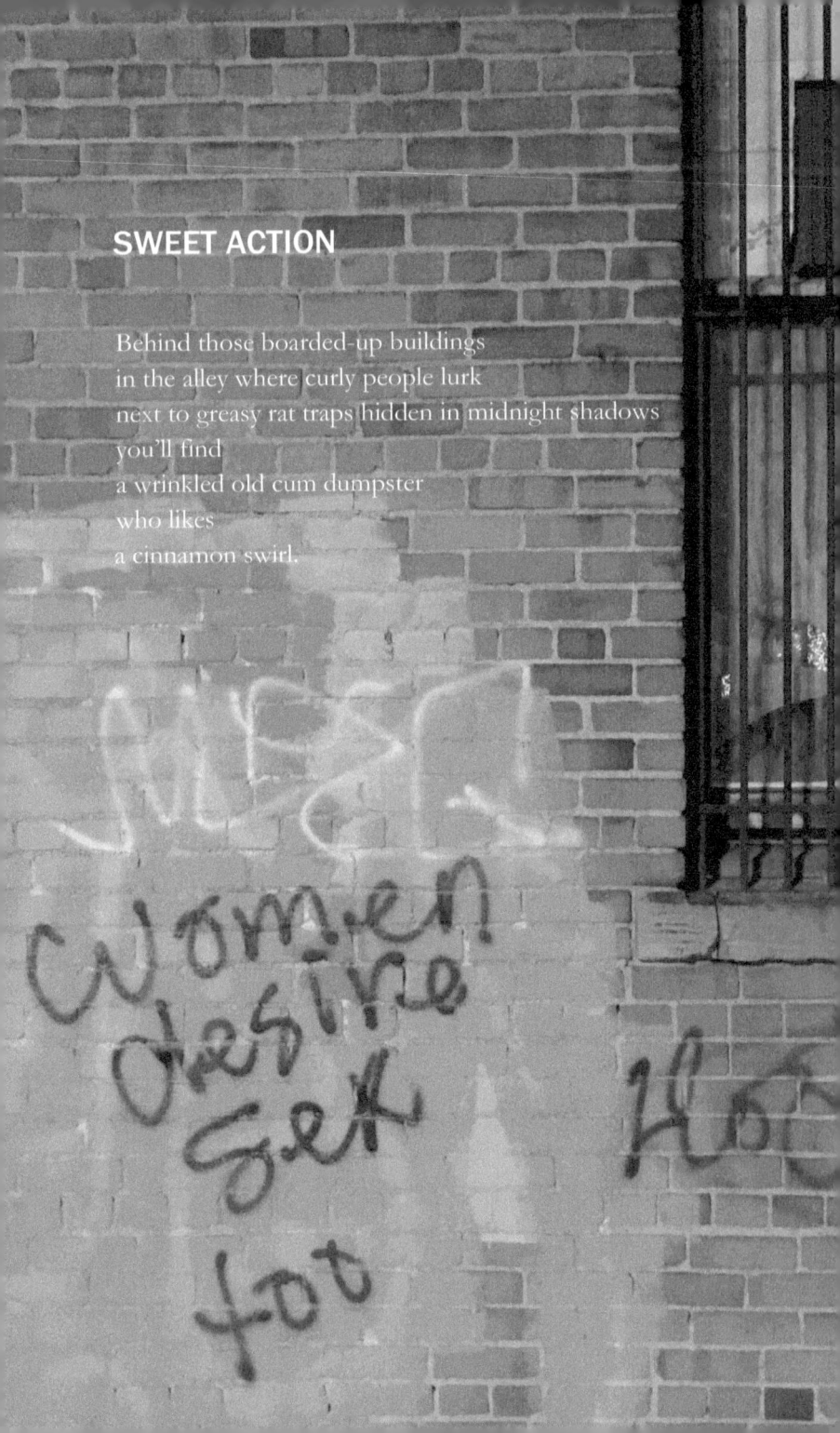

SWEET ACTION

Behind those boarded-up buildings
in the alley where curly people lurk
next to greasy rat traps hidden in midnight shadows
you'll find
a wrinkled old cum dumpster
who likes
a cinnamon swirl.

YOU GOT OPTIONS

Option 1: You wait to die and *Justice with Judge Jesus* replays wha' happn'd to you all those times you were blackout drunk.

Option 2: Rub my crystal balls and I'll show you right now.

So which will it be?

Ahhhhhhhh … good choice. Yeah, that feels really nice.

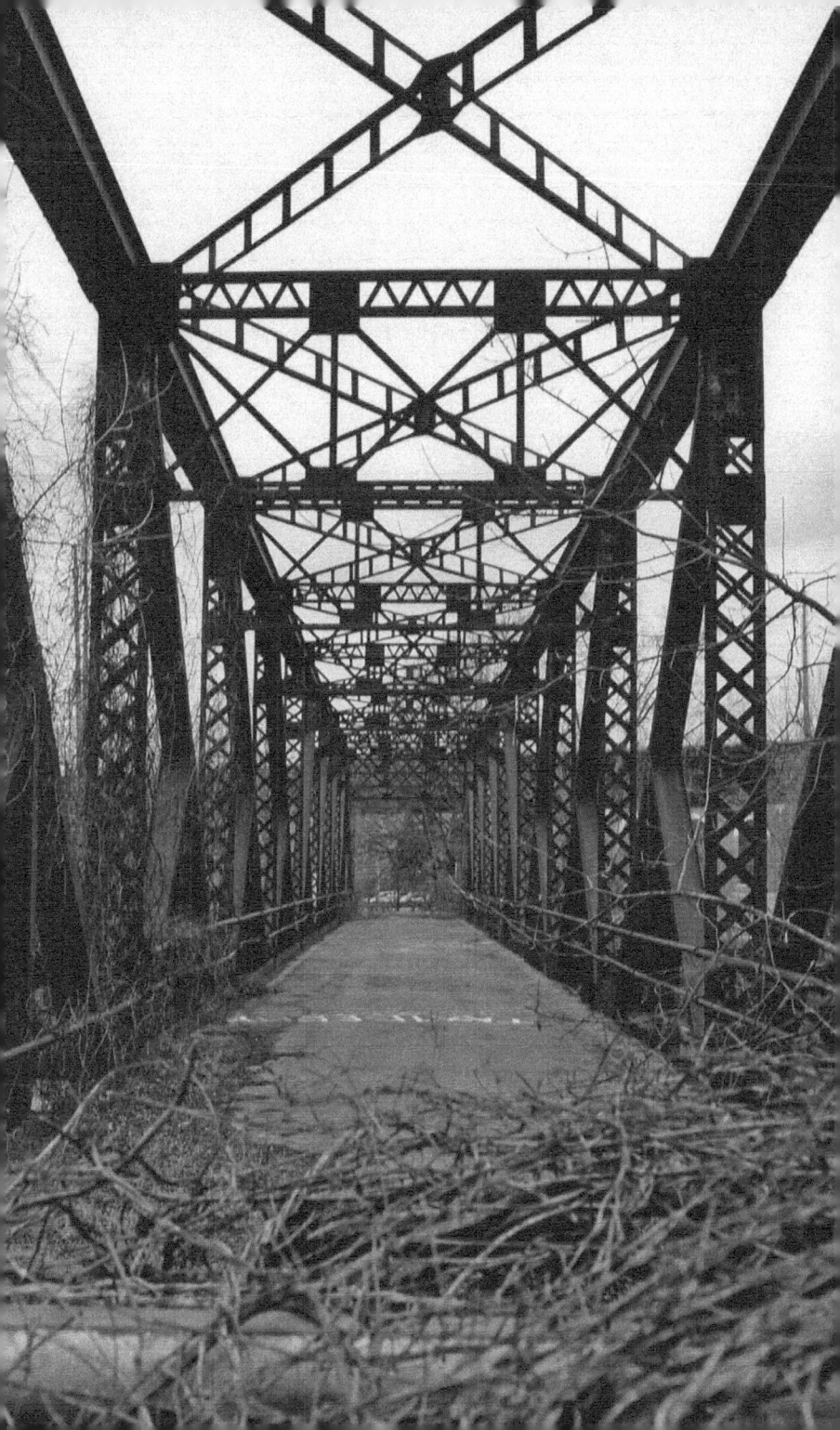

R-E-S-P-E-C-T
HER
U-R-E-T-H-R-A

There is a difference between a
BAR
and a
BATHROOM

Treat a women's urethra with respect

... also R.I.P. $coot Doo

BE MINE

Crushing & snorting a whole bag of candy hearts
to get the party started.
Swinging nun chucks in her front yard
like Cobra Kai cool.
She won't answer
but I know she's gotta be watching
through her tiny peep hole
cos I'm feelin' sexy,
so sexy that my
flaming skulls club shirt
is literally
ON FIRE.
Ohhhh, but my balls is aching
& mouth be begging
for just another squirt
of her animalizing
pussy juice.

Yet somehow
the night
always ends with
cops
&
new bruises.

DESCENDER OF "HELL"

In the downtown library men's room,
spinning whole rolls till their spun,
one stall to the next,
cursed
by a messy
never ending
beer shit.

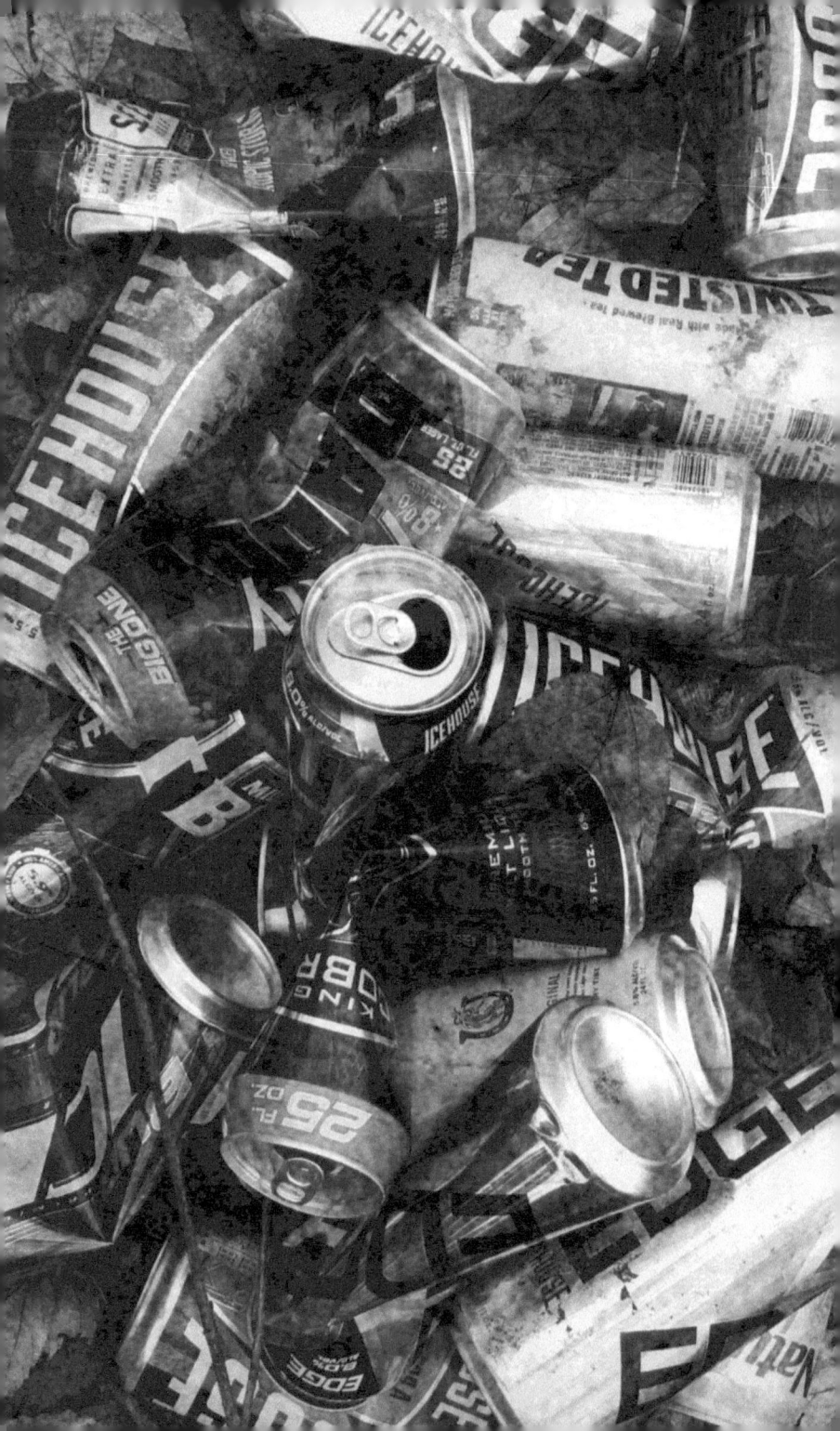

NIGHT FREAKS

The moon
will rise
again.

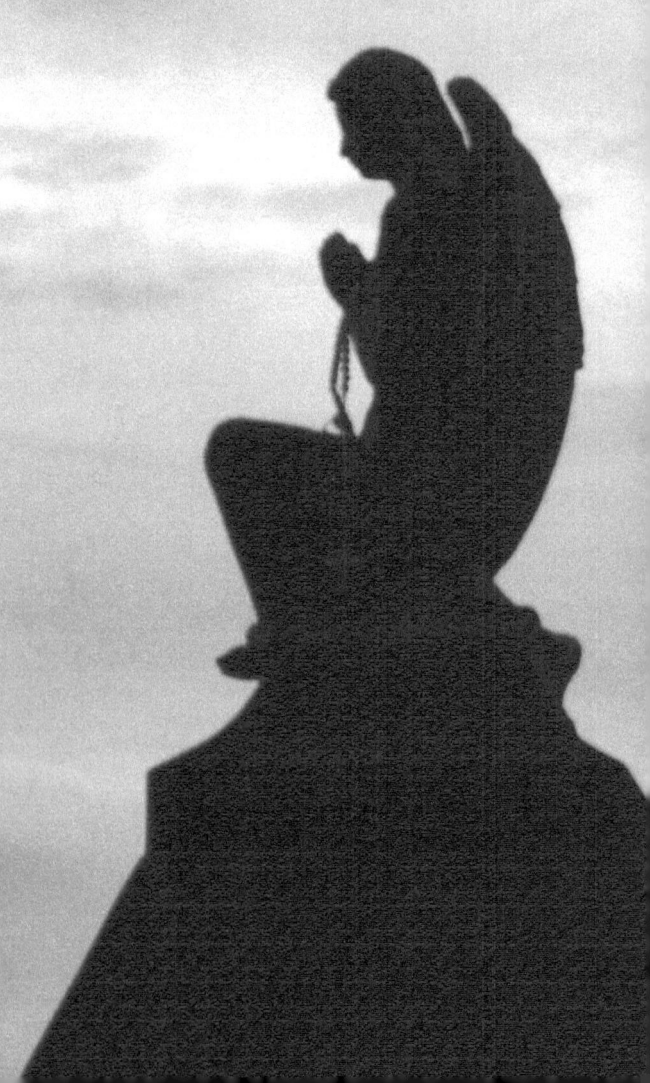

NOT TO BE CONFUSED WITH LYRICS FROM THE GREAT WHITE SONG "ONCE BITTEN TWICE SHY"

Punch boys
in their
jaw
if they
put
their
jaws
on
your
pu$$y

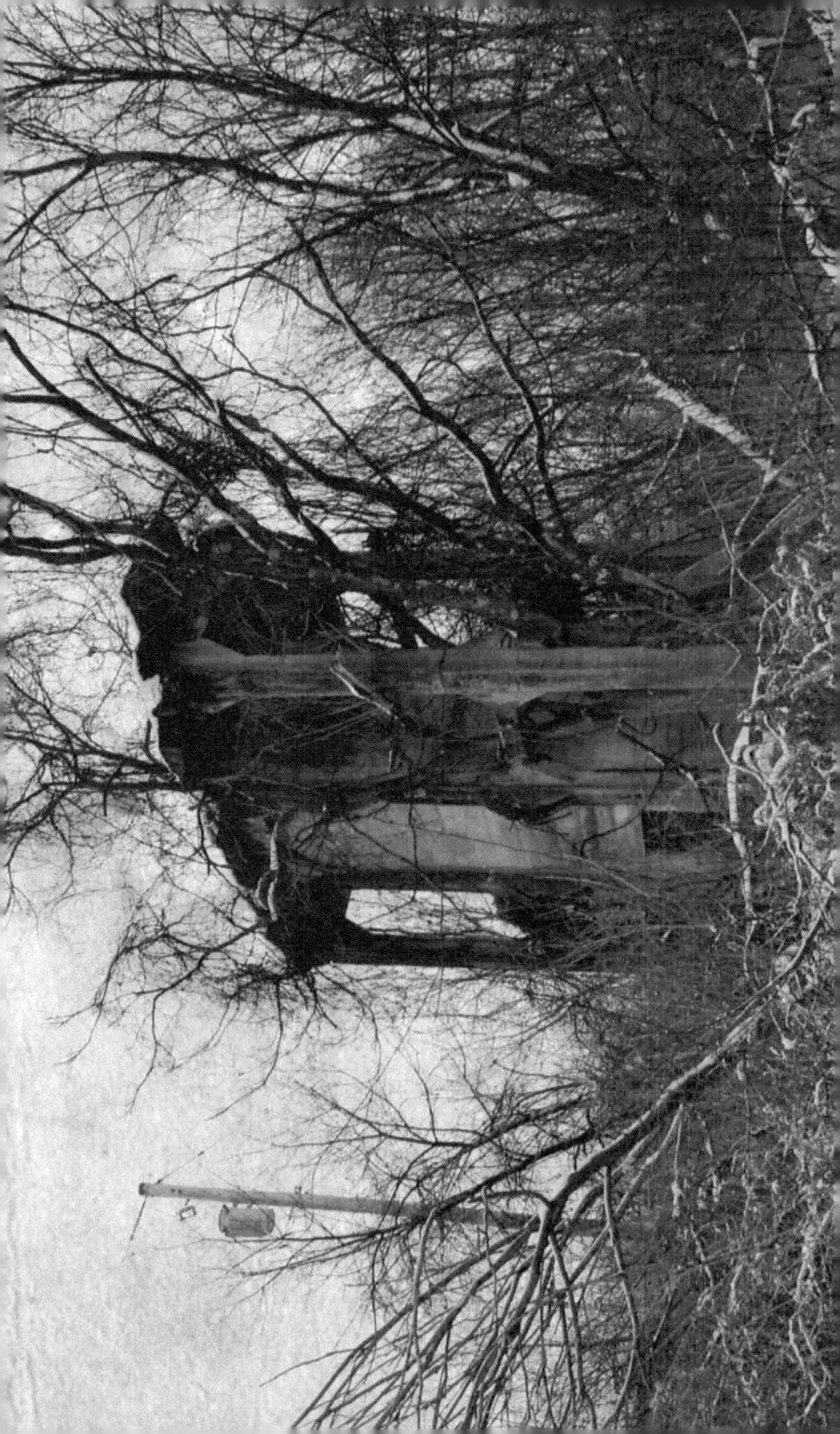

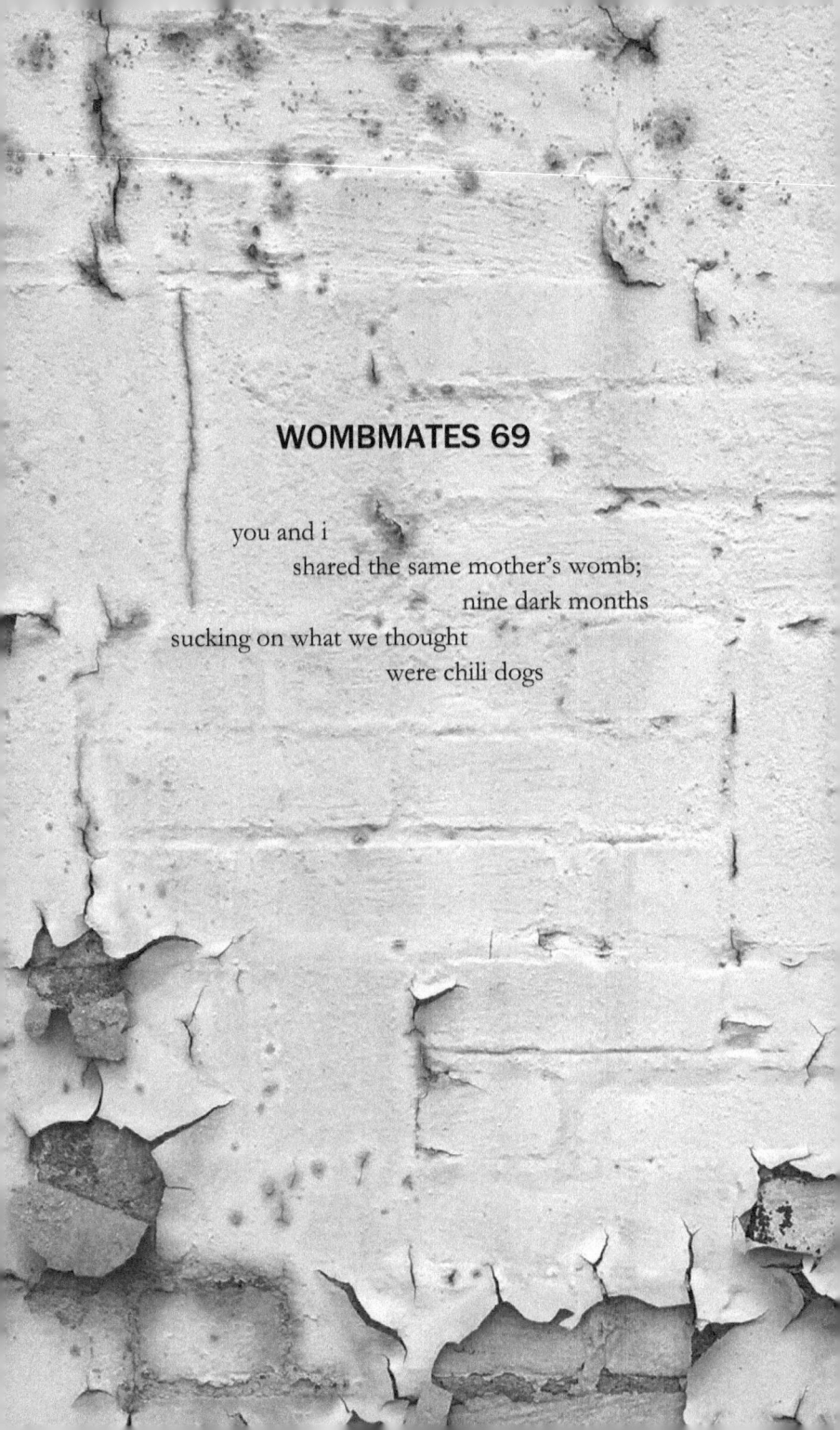

WOMBMATES 69

you and i
 shared the same mother's womb;
  nine dark months
sucking on what we thought
 were chili dogs

WILLY'S WONKA

She tickled Willy's wonka
in a K-Mart parking lot.

"That's how we play," she kept repeating to me.

I about
choked
on
my
Everlasting
Gobbstopper
before
spitting it out
and leaving her
for
good.

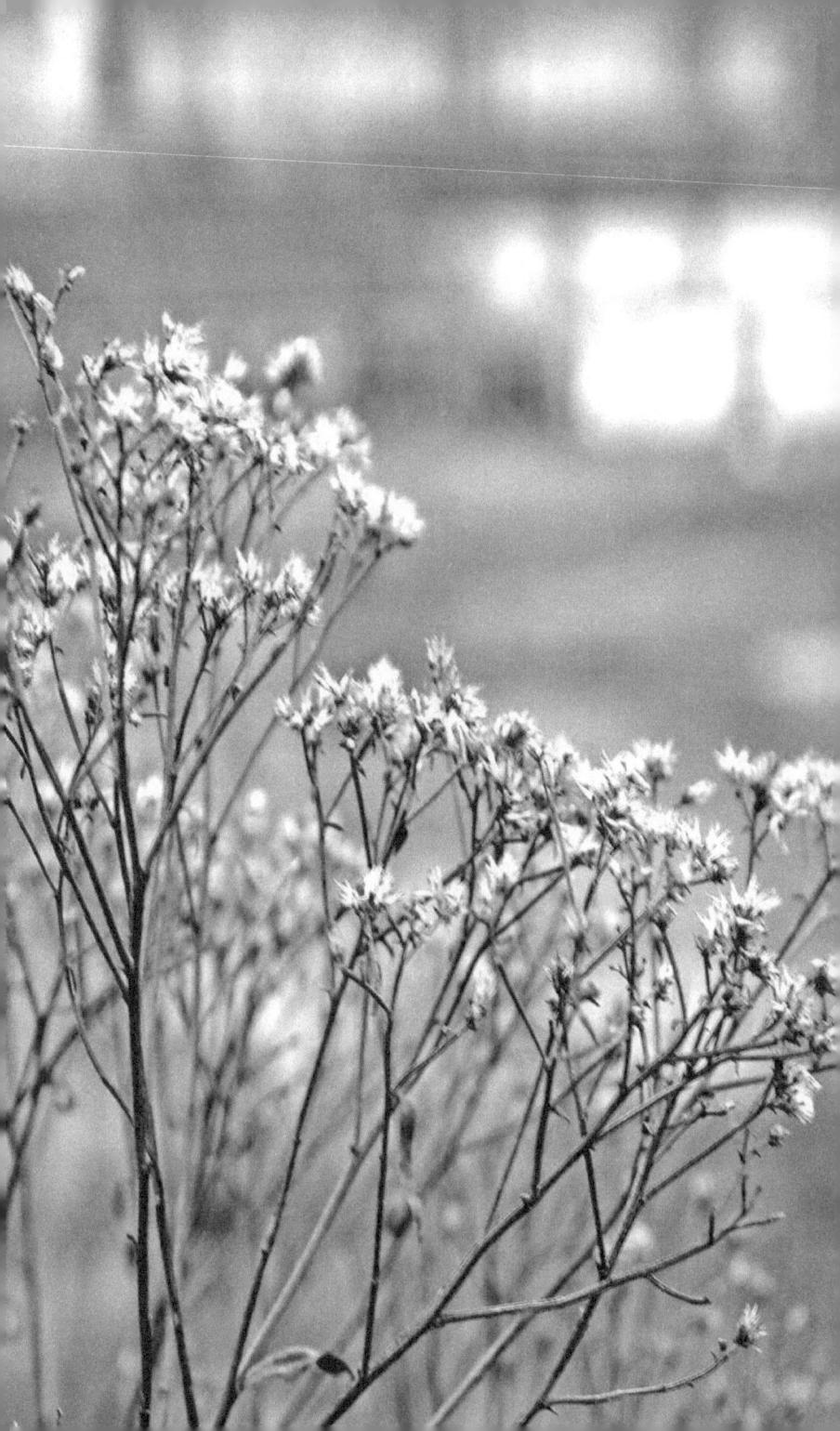

ROCKET RIDE

Eddie
Loves
Debbie
Always
Forever
And
Eternally

To the moon and back a 1,000,000,000,000 times infinity

WILD PARTY ANIMAL

The mud-covered carcass of a raccoon
reaching up to heaven
on the side of the road
with a helium-inflated mylar Happy Birthday balloon
tied to his left leg,
but the balloon only bobs in the wind
of each speeding passerby automobile
instead of lifting the road kill
away.

KNOCK KNOCK

If she knocks
on your
door,
it means
she wants to
slob
on your
knob.

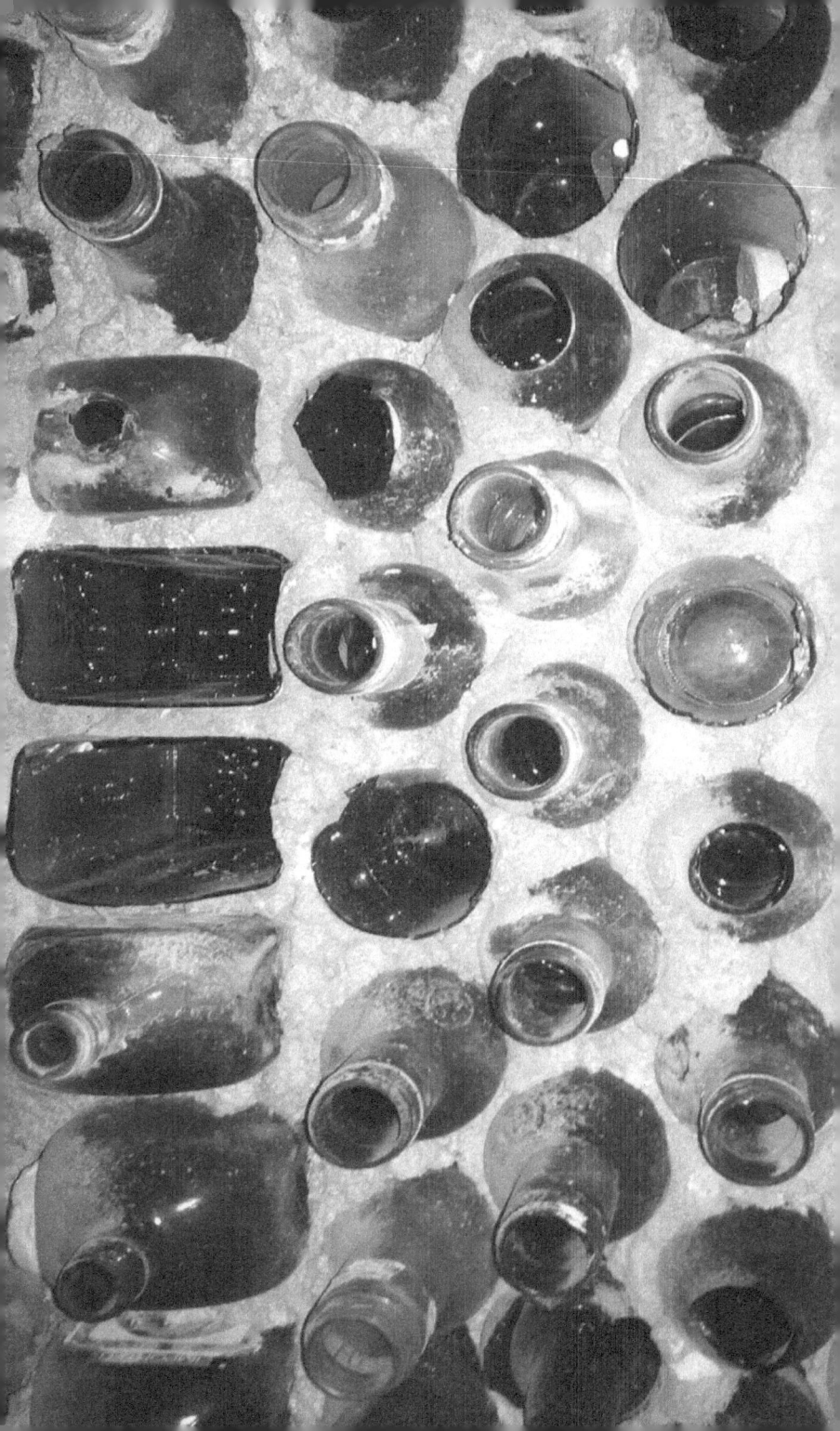

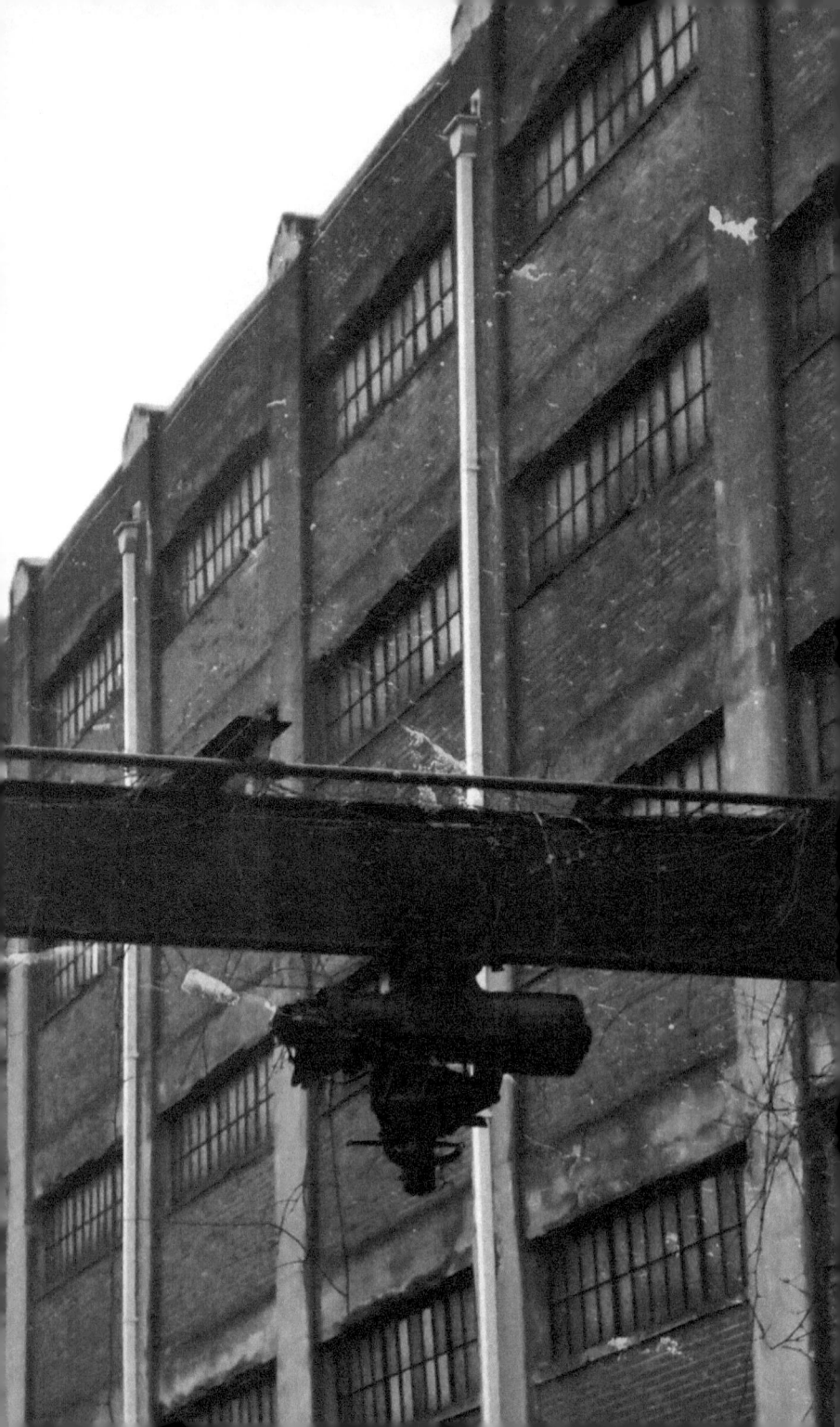

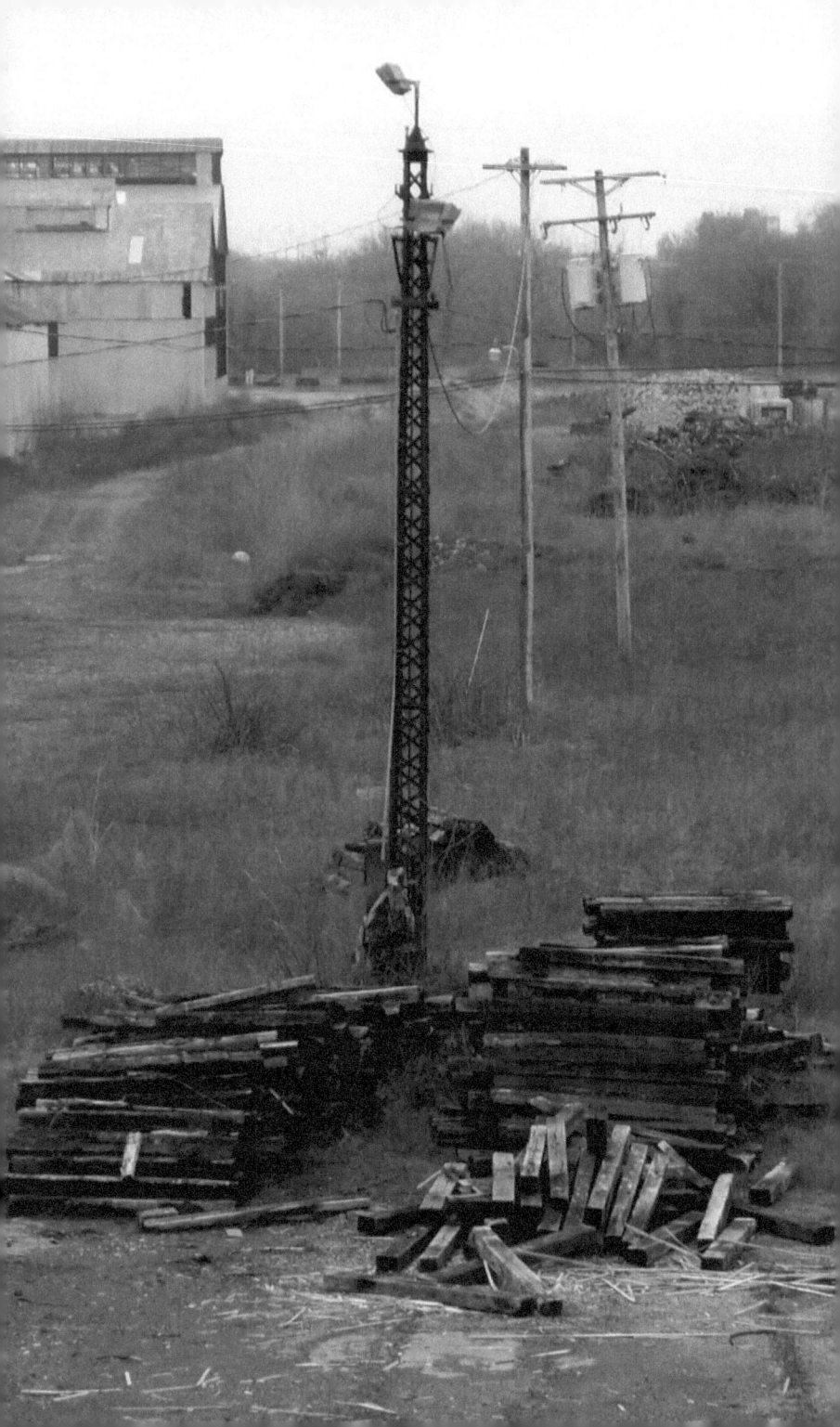

LAYING EGGS IN THE SHOWER

Sometimes I'll lay an egg in the shower
and a little pee comes out afterward
but it's okay because I wear socks.

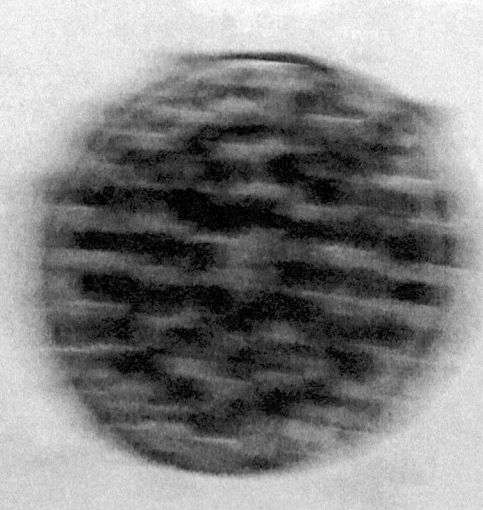

PEOPLE V. THE SNEAKY POOPER

Was evicted after
Justice with Judge Larry found me guilty
for using my neighbor's bidet toilet while he was gone
which flooded multiple floors of the building
which destroyed multiple apartments
which everyone hates me for now
which means people are trying to kill me
which means I'm always on the run
which means I need to find the alien portal down by the river
that will take me to the 4th Dimension
and I can be like,
"Bye, bitches."

I WANT 2 BELIEVE

1.

Down in the river bed dried after a flood, I trudge among washed up water bottles, liquor bottles, ketchup bottles, motor oil bottles, soda bottles, beer bottles, beer cans, and everything else like that (and not like that—I mean like woods stuff and bigger garbage stuff like broken plastic chairs and empty fire extinguishers), searching for the alien portal to the 4th Dimension.

I swear the portal's got to be real because a few weeks ago I was fucking around down there trying to catch a fish and half my body started getting sucked into it. But I was too afraid to let it take me and fought my way free.

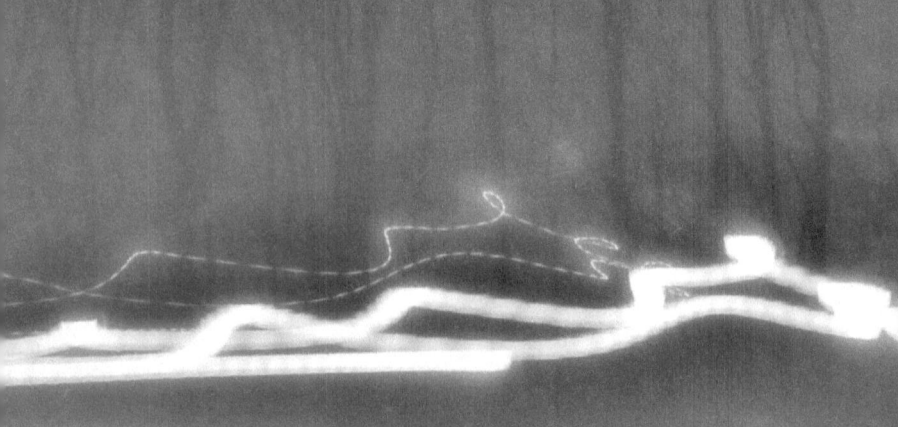

2.

Apparently a dude who works at the Burger King on 3rd Street went missing a month ago. There's a photo on his Facebook page of his warped body in the portal. According to his dad's comments he's still missing. And according to comments from other people, the dad works at the same Burger King. Furthermore, his mom works there too. Even furthermore, his 97-year-old grandma as well. How fucking weird is that?

(Library only lets me use the computer for 2 hours each day; that's never enough time to investigate alien portals.
And I'm still waiting for Obama to give me a free iPhone, so … thanks, Obama.)

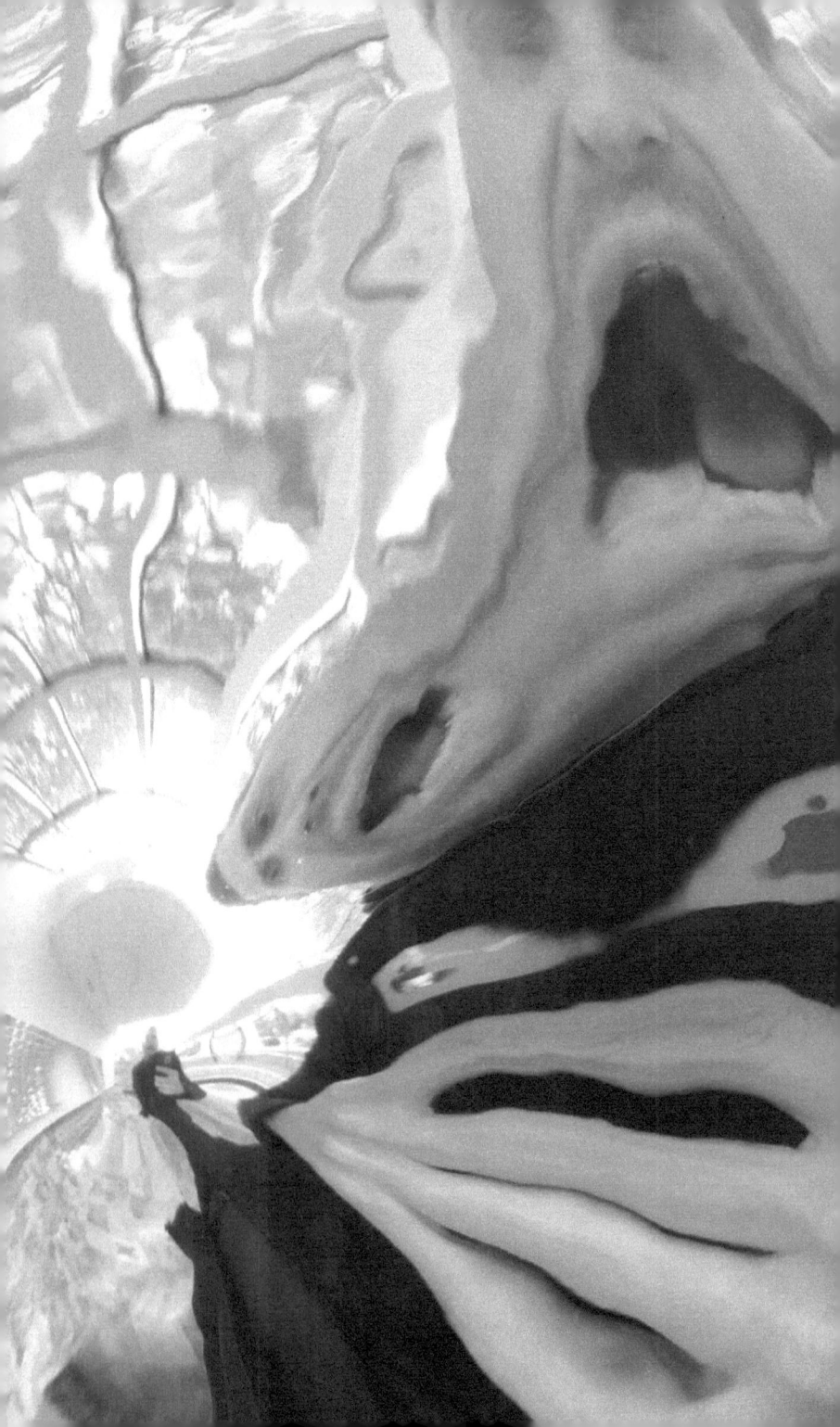

3.

I just laid another egg in the shower and I hope this one finally has a baby alien in it who can open the portal.

To Be Continued.

HOW THE WESTSIDE WAS WON

Word is Billy the Kid
shot
Jose (the self-proclaimed) #1 Mexican
after Jose
stole
Billy's
cock ring.

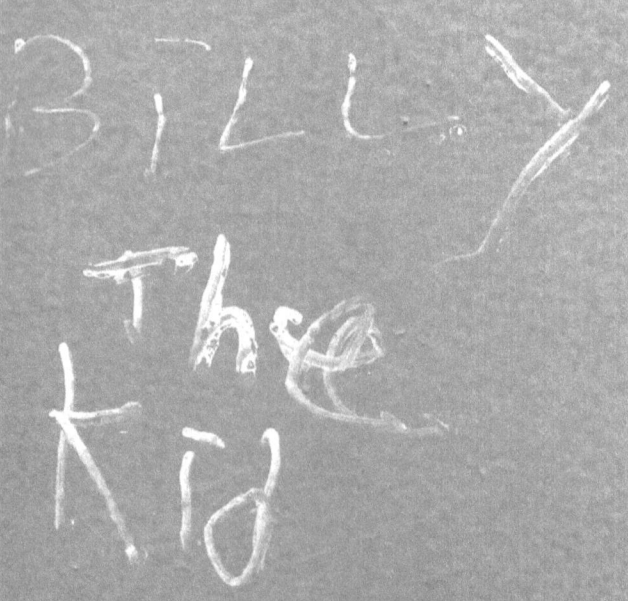

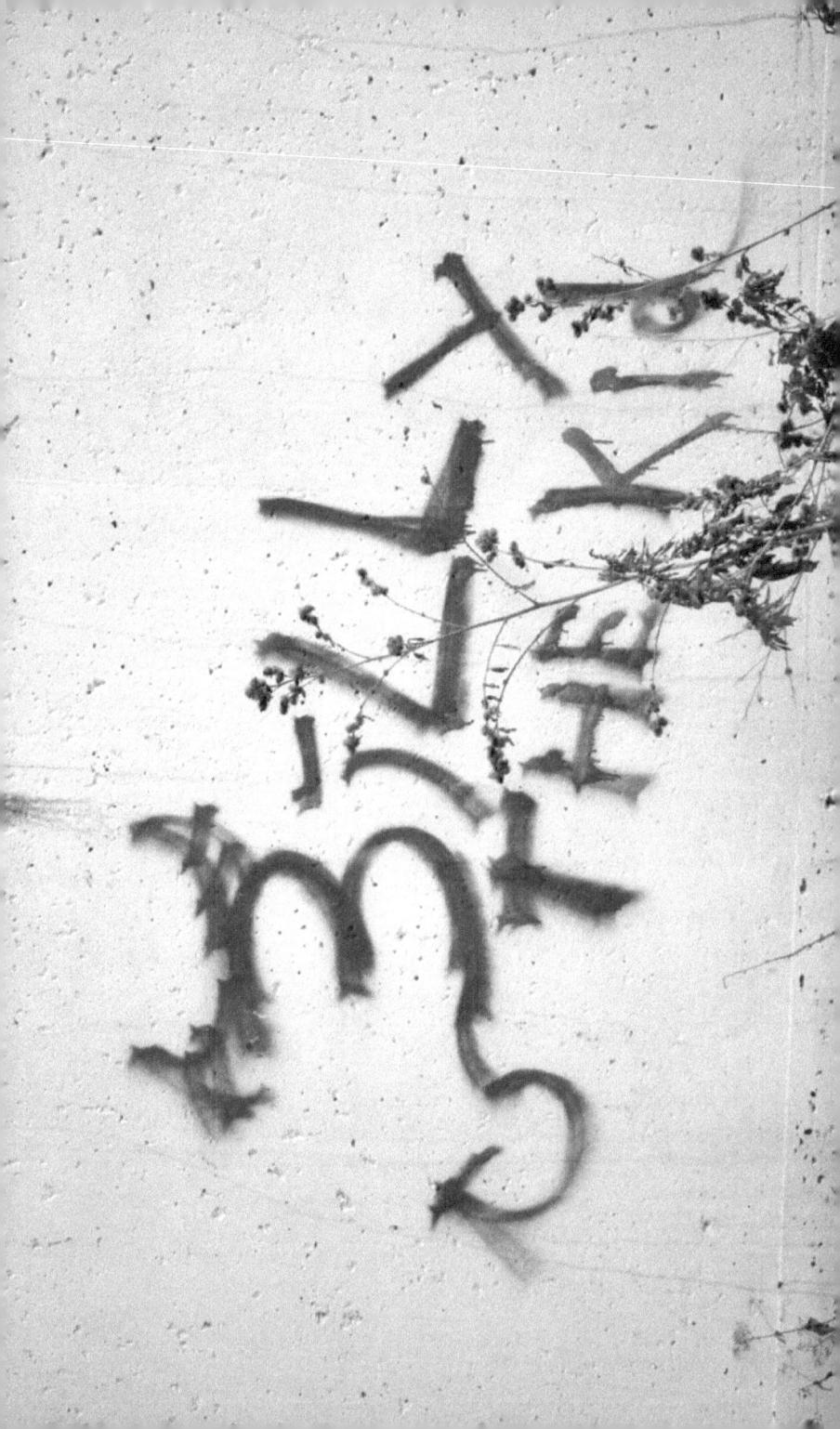

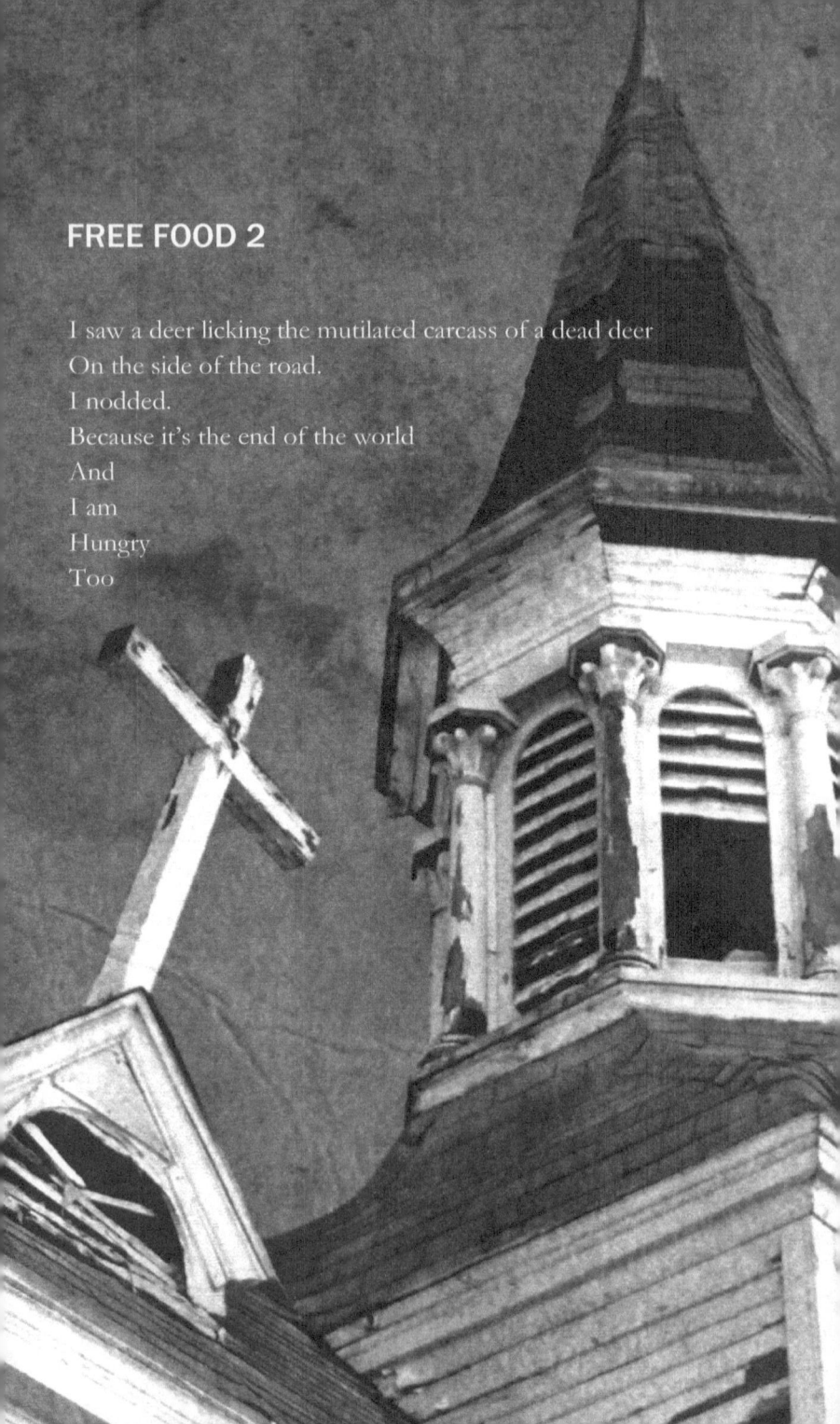

FREE FOOD 2

I saw a deer licking the mutilated carcass of a dead deer
On the side of the road.
I nodded.
Because it's the end of the world
And
I am
Hungry
Too

MY FIRST HAIRCUT

I don't remember my first haircut, but I remember the time last week when I snuck into an unlocked and empty Holiday Inn banquet hall to sleep on their lobby sofa. Woke up in the middle of the night, itched my scalp, and pulled out from my knotted hair a tiny Virgin Mary with a missing left hand giving birth to a baby 40 oz. malt liquor bottle.

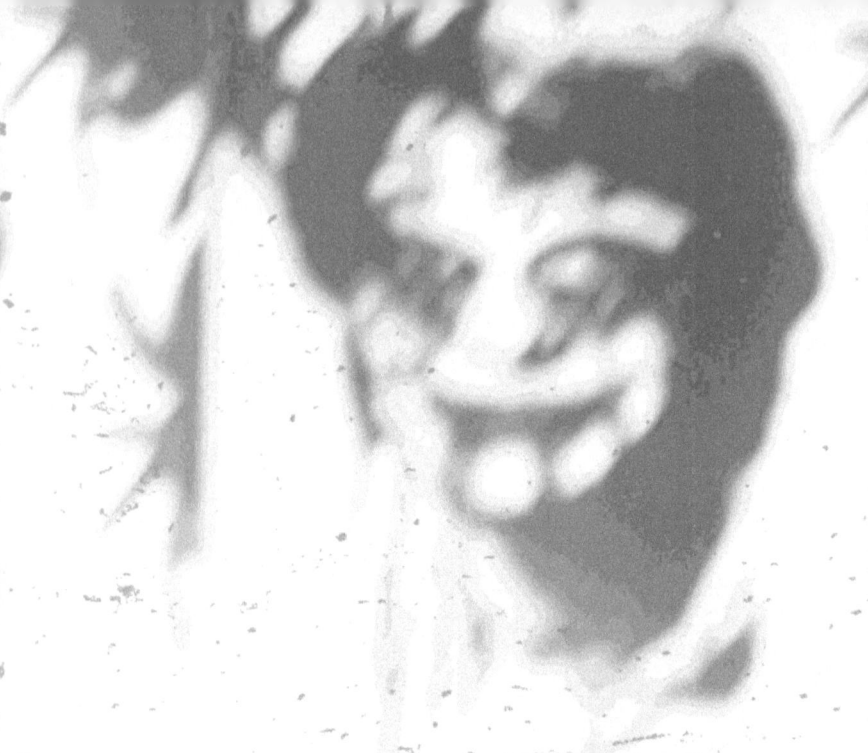

ONLINE EMPLOYMENT APPLICATION Q.1: HOW WOULD YOU DESCRIBE YOURSELF?

I would say I am a cross between a tarantula and Alex Keaton from the '80s sitcom *Family Ties*.

ONLINE EMPLOYMENT APPLICATION Q.2: WHY DO YOU WANT TO WORK AT ▮▮▮▮?

'Cause it's like what that little Mexican dude down in North Carolina told me—the guy I had a dream about seeing with his pants down, holding his thing in his hand, a weird thing that looked like a flailing night crawler worm, and I thought that was a really sick thing to dream about, and I never wanted to see him in person afterward (or in my dreams again), and I still don't know what that dream means because I love tits, pussy, and ass. Anyway, the little amigo said, "No money, no honey." He said that in perfect English. Then he told me you were hiring, so ….

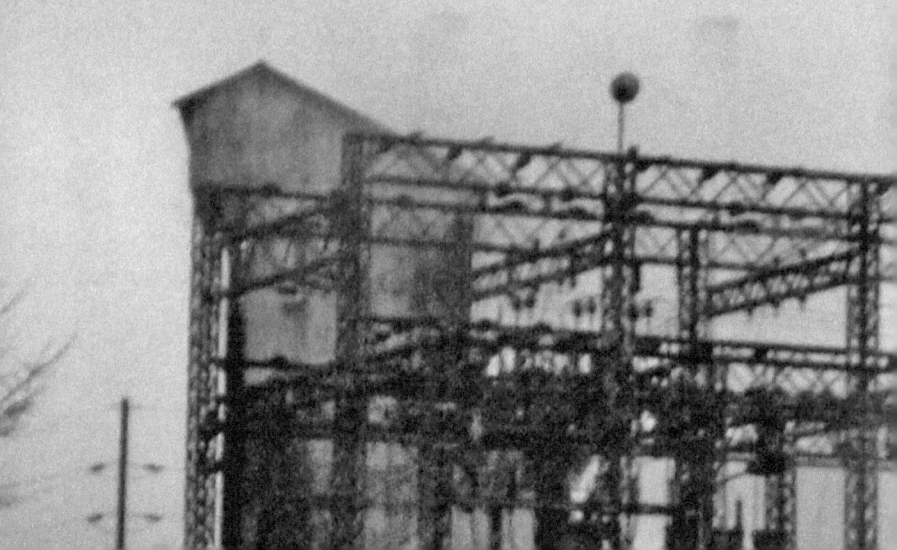

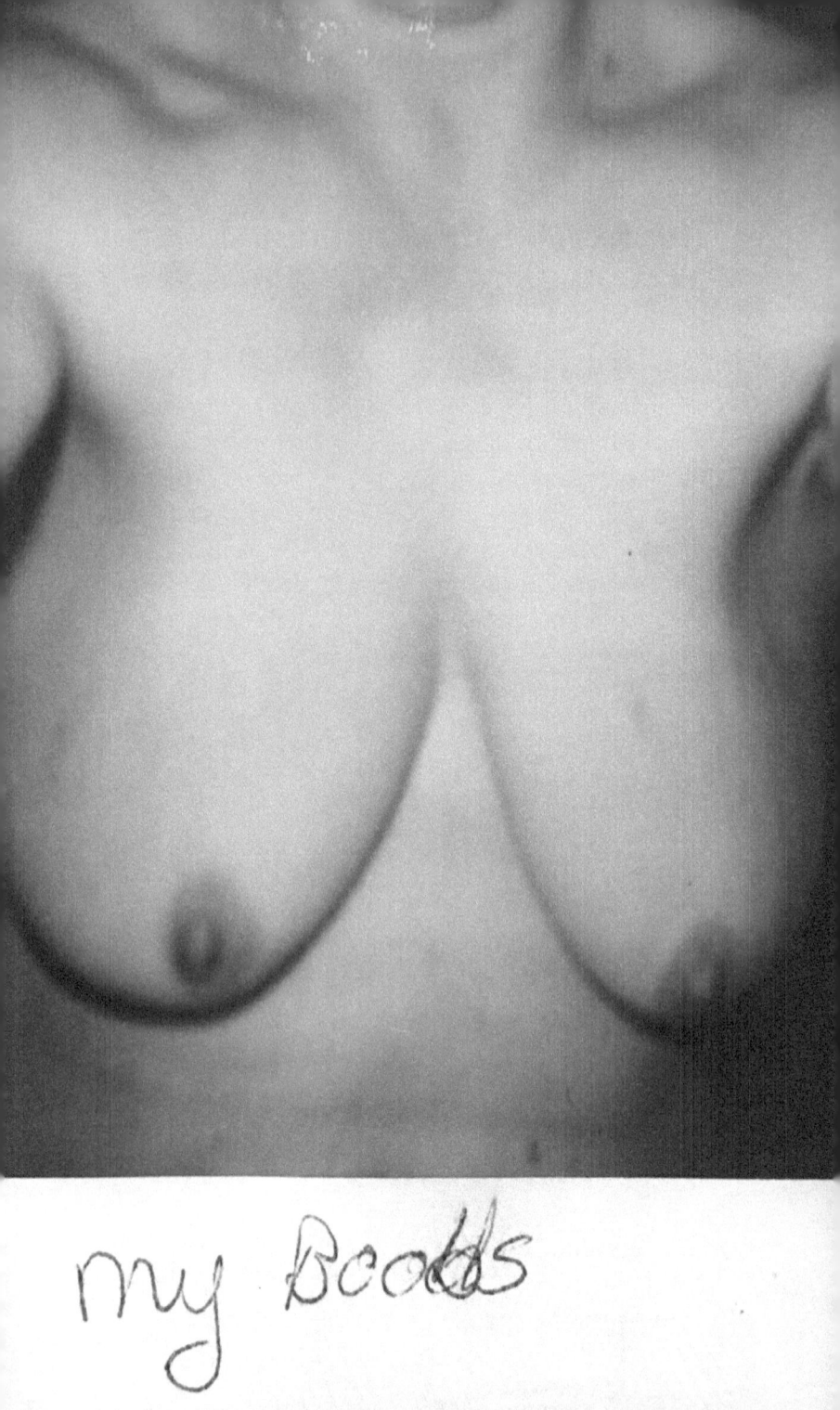

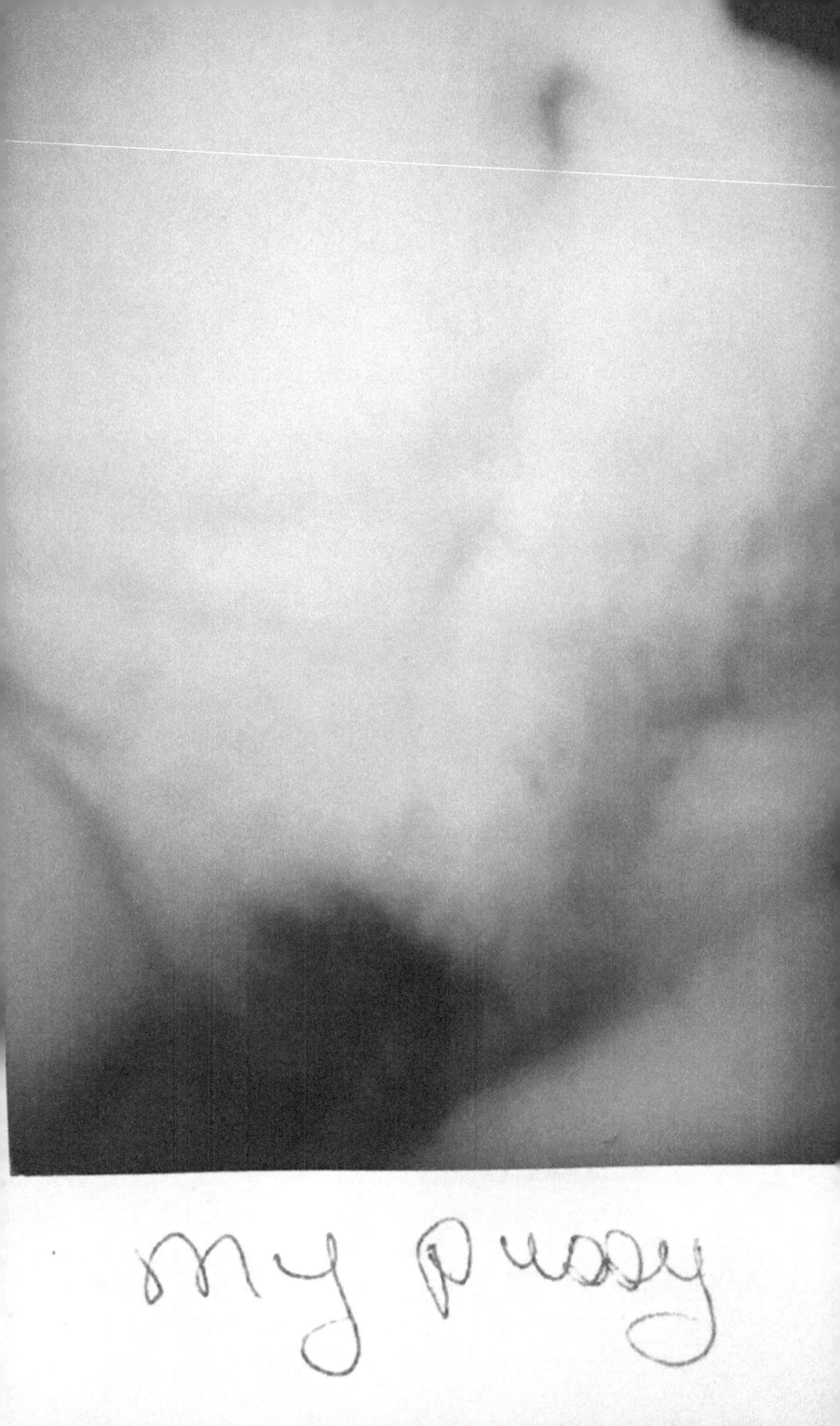

BOO HOO

for a few months
I had a ghost girlfriend named Greta who
lived far away in a weird land only reachable by boat
could grow a thin black Sharpie mustache
bathed in a tub of books
plucked math equations from trees and ate them like fruit
had an internet voice louder than a leaf blower
wore a red cloak of fungi to worship Satan in the forest
had no car
rode the city train
eventually left me
to marry an artistic guy who had a real mustache and
gave her
half of his.

HARD TIMES

Hard times
Hold on

Hard times
Let go

Hard times
Who knows?

Hard times
Have your case settled
on *Justice with Judge Jesus*

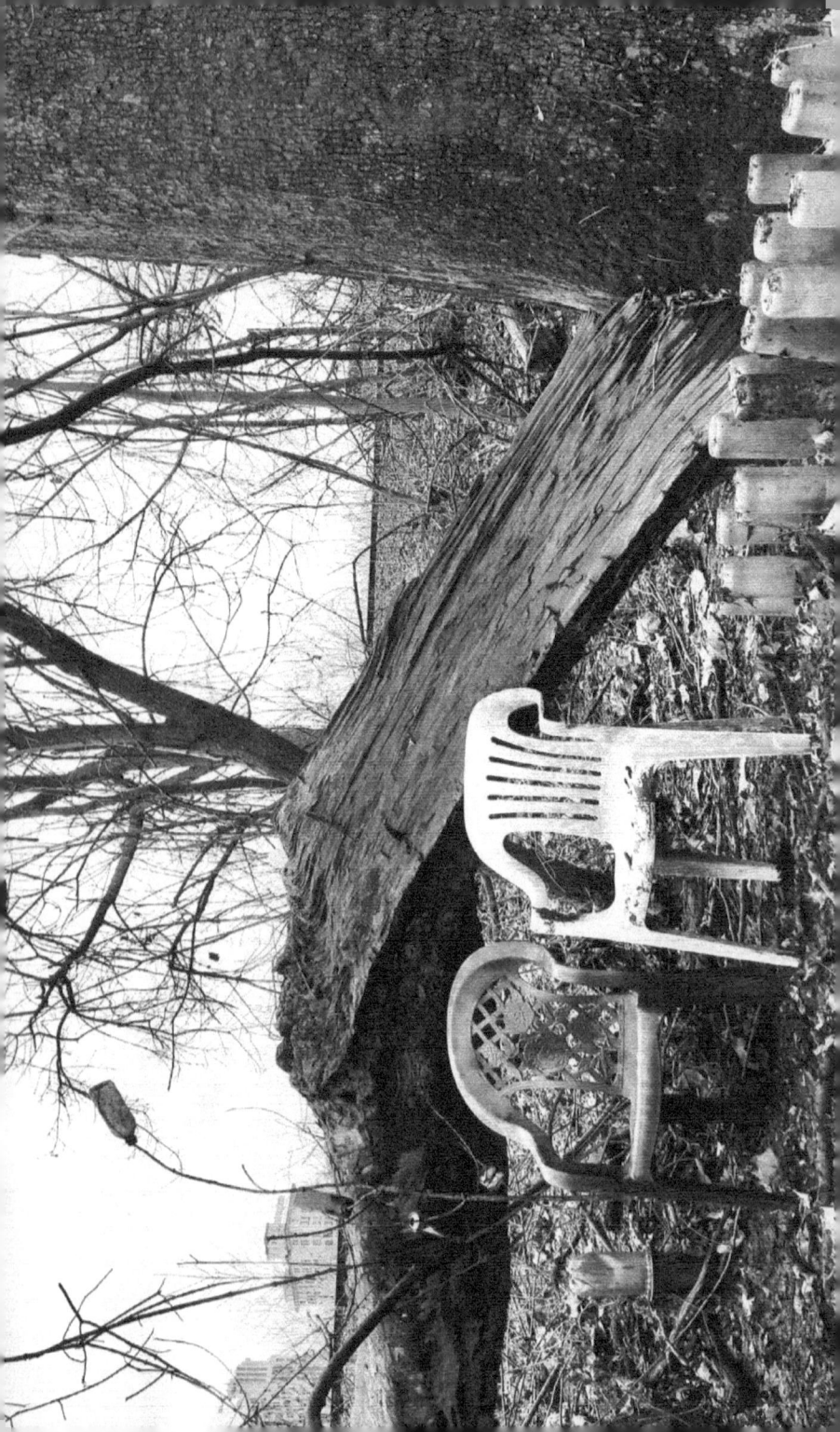

GC THE GPK

GARY Coleman
wuz my favorite
Garbage Pail Kid.

FREE FOOD 3

A city closed on
Sunday
makes me wait under 5th Street Bridge
for the miracle of another
white styrofoam to go box
filled with hot food
to appear before me;
its contents held safely in a white plastic bag
with white paper napkins
and white plastic utensils
like it's happened many times before.
But it's always after
my stomach hears the church bells ring
that Saint Styrofoam's joyous tongue sings:
"Oh whatta wonderful day!"
And then
Bang!
It's hello Slobber Day.

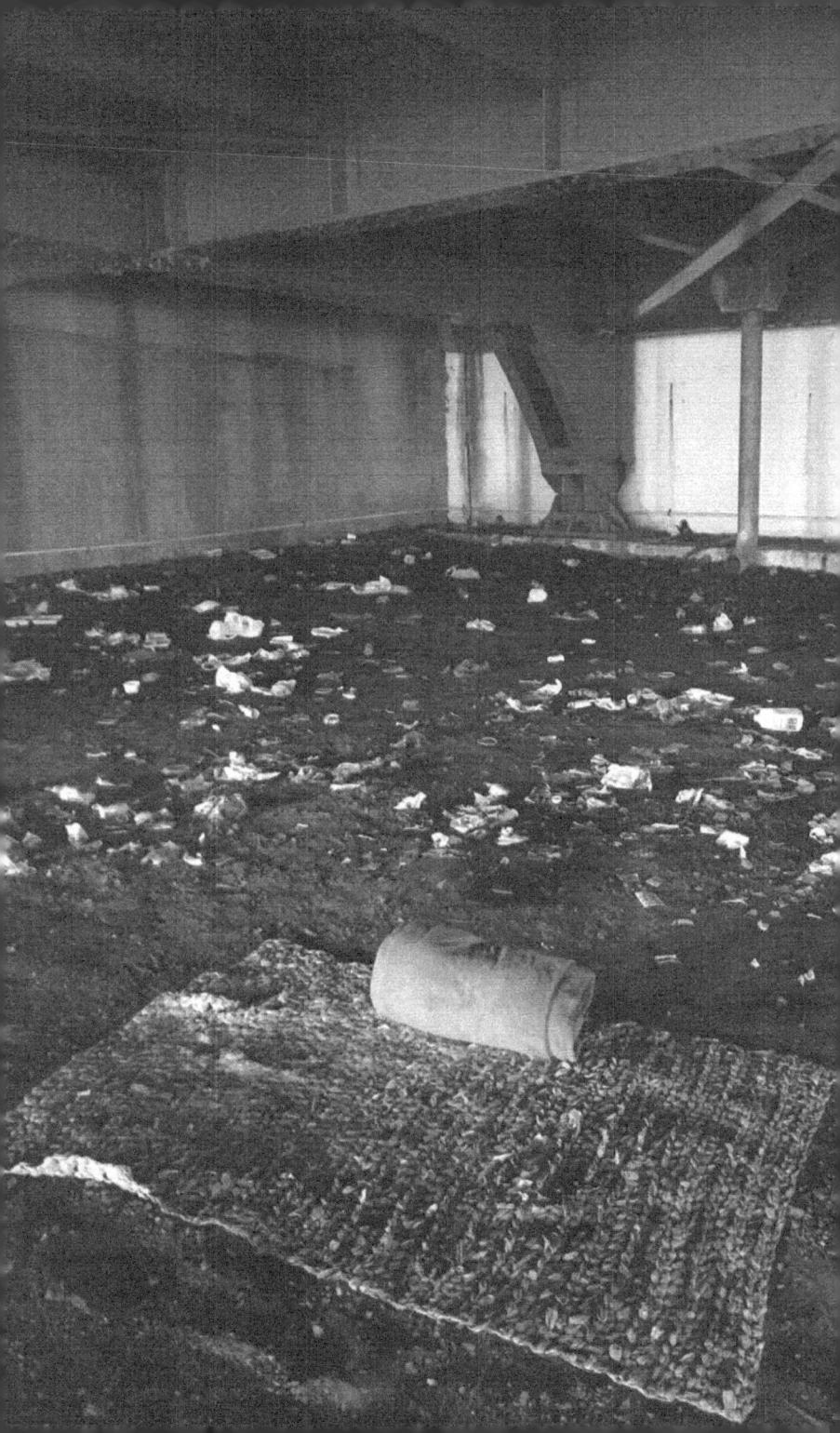

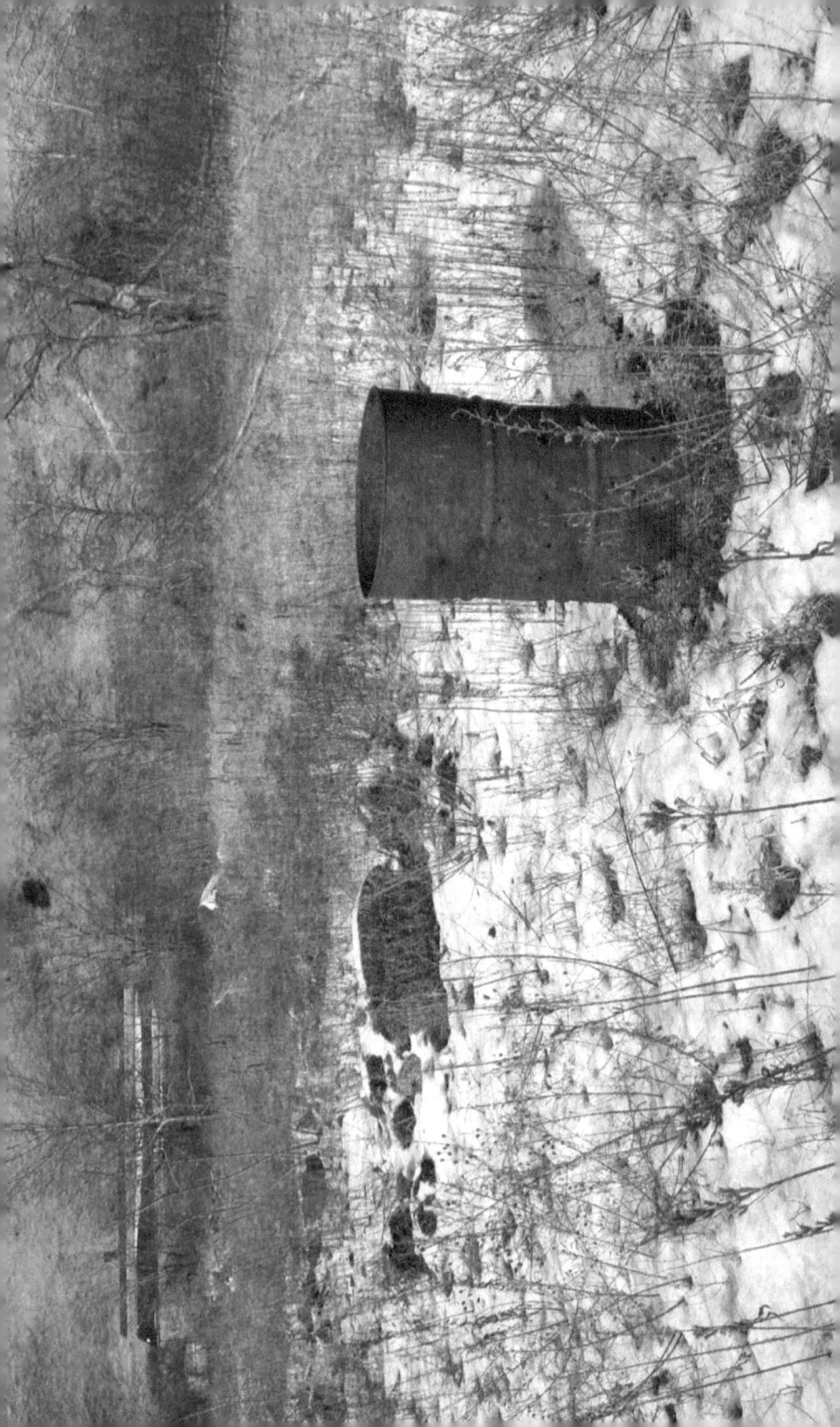

CHILLING WITH OLIVE STRANGE

Olive Strange is her real name?
She hugs her black cat named Hong Kong 1999
and tells me this cat is her little
baked potato.

Olive Strange might be her code name
because she never removes her neon green ski mask
even while she strips for me in the Taco Bell parking lot
in the dark
in the back seat of her old Hyundai Sonata.

What's also strange
is she wants me to squirt my fire sauce into a paper wrapper
instead of inside her
delicious taco.

Even though I obey,
one of these days
I want Olive Strange
to bake me a potato
that
we can name
Operation Desert Storm.

LOOK AT THAT ... BLUETOOTH

This carpenter guy I know
showed me how to skin the bark
off a certain kind of living tree
with a sharp knife,
strip it bare.
What we'd find is a
glowing bright blue flesh he'd
tell me is
bluetooth.

I went around skinning a lot of
trees after that.
But I didn't need a knife;
I could do it with
my mind.

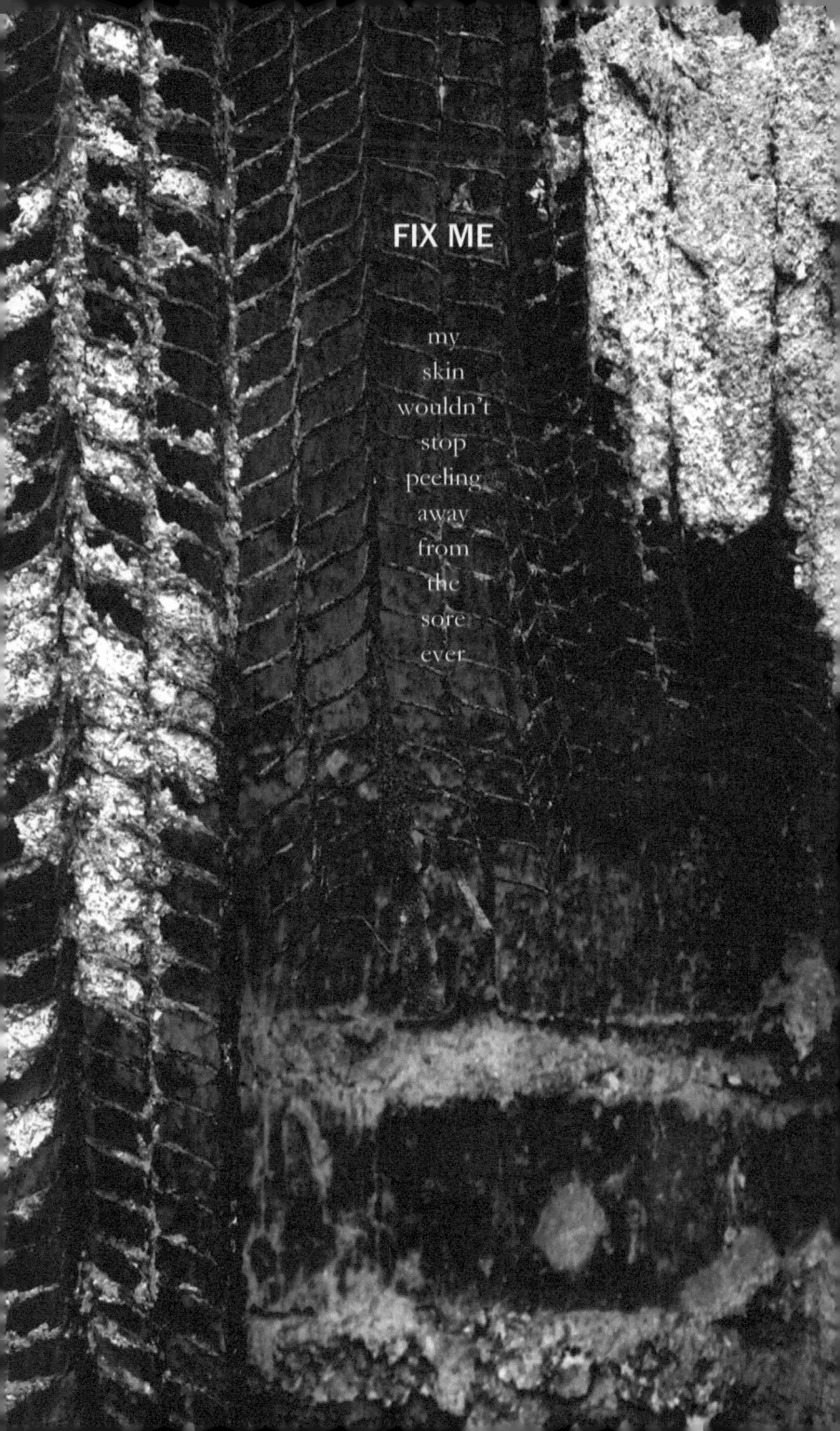

WHERE THE SKELETONS ARE

It was nearing dusk when I ventured into the derelict warehouse
following a guy wearing a backpack.

Inside was lined in rows of single-person brass beds. Some accompanied wooden nightstands and dim lamps lighting skeleton residents lying atop their bed as if in a coffin.

I approached a skeleton who wore a country flower print red and white dress, fascinated by the dress's pristine condition.

Then the guy with the backpack picked up her skull and put it in his backpack—I couldn't believe he did that.

The examination began at the hotel room. It was discovered that the skull had a bullet hole in the bottom of its jaw.

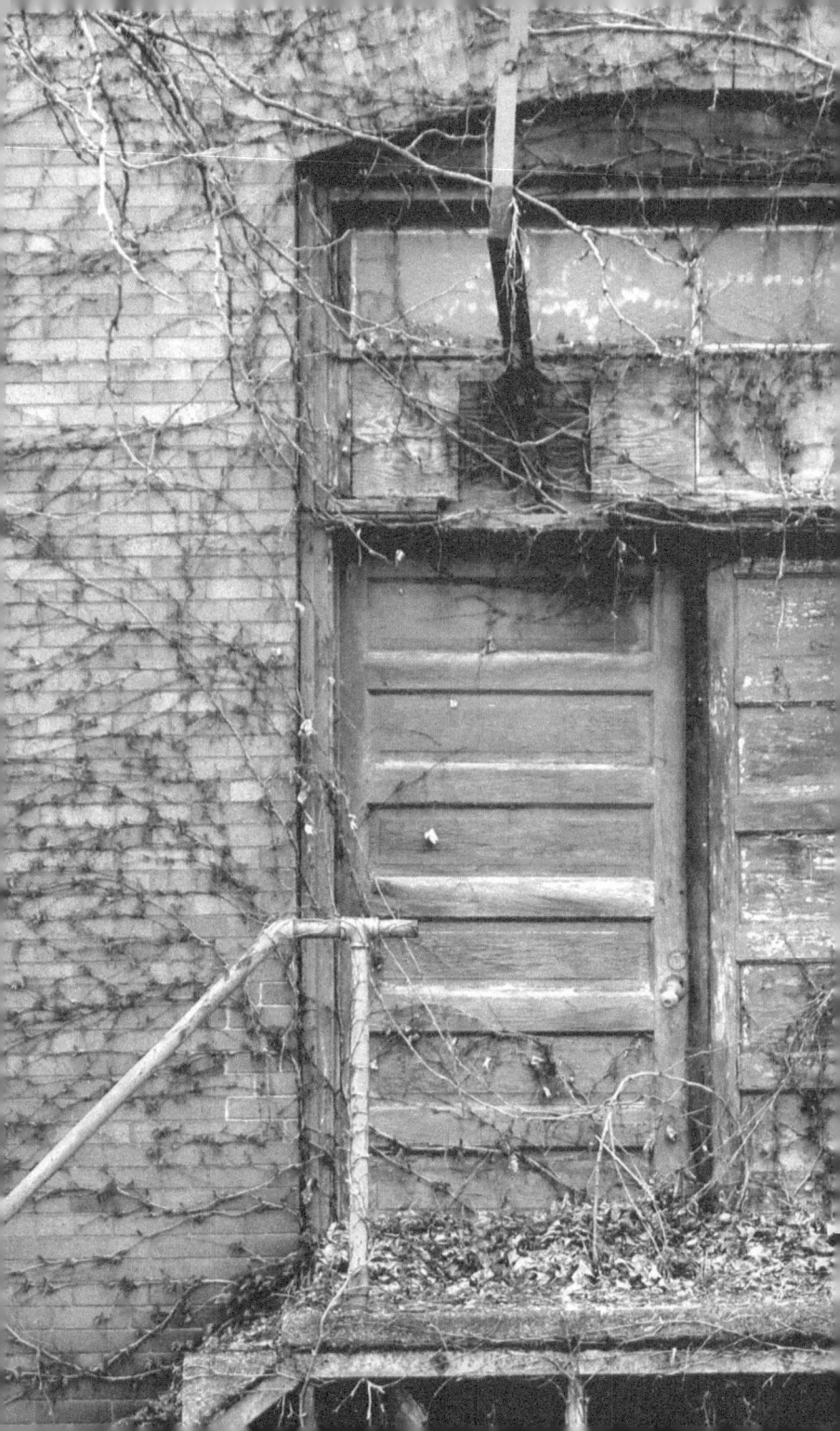

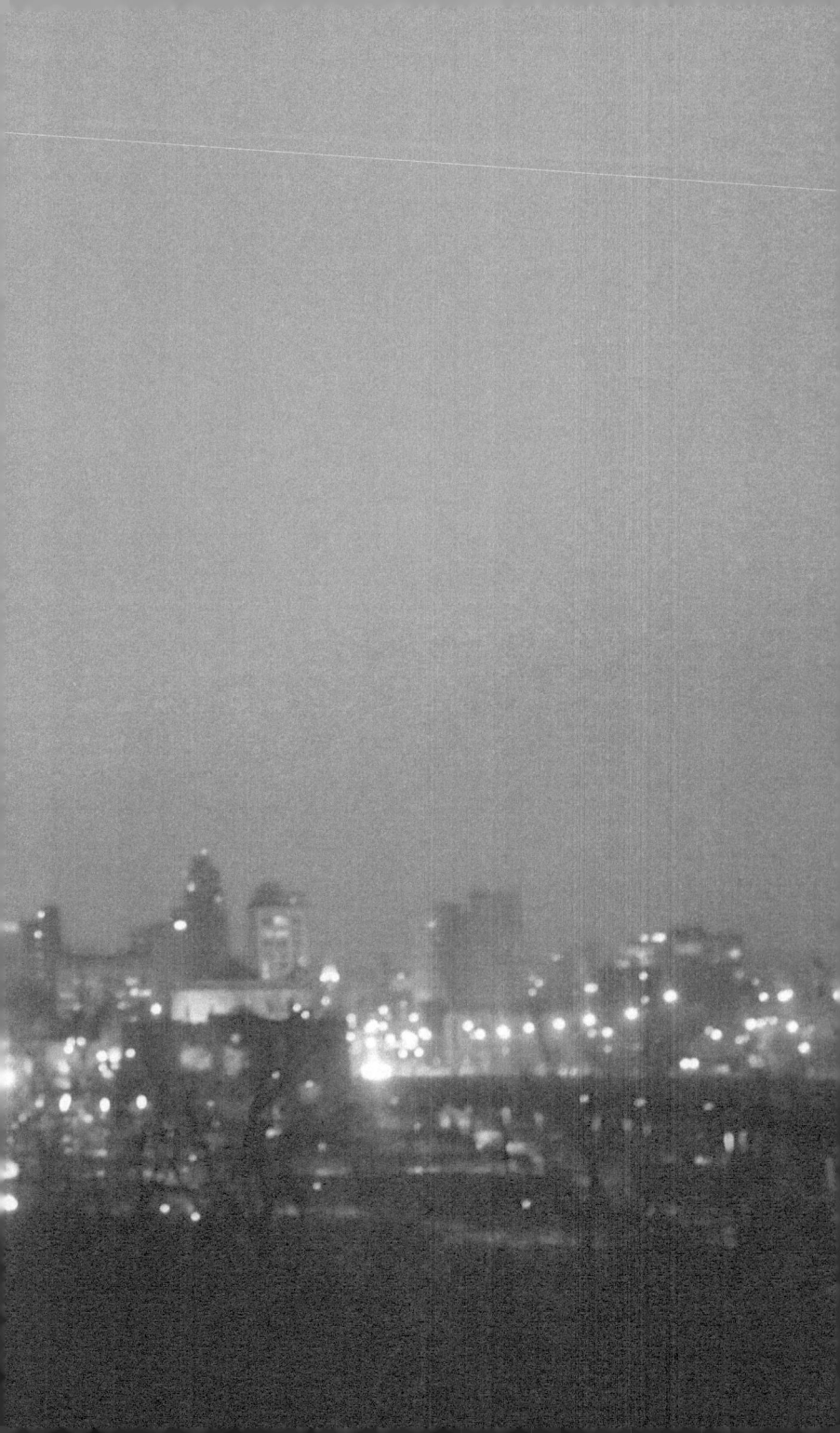

Eddie
Loves
Debbie

Strala
Poka
Isa
Lover
her
Kenny
works
on
car

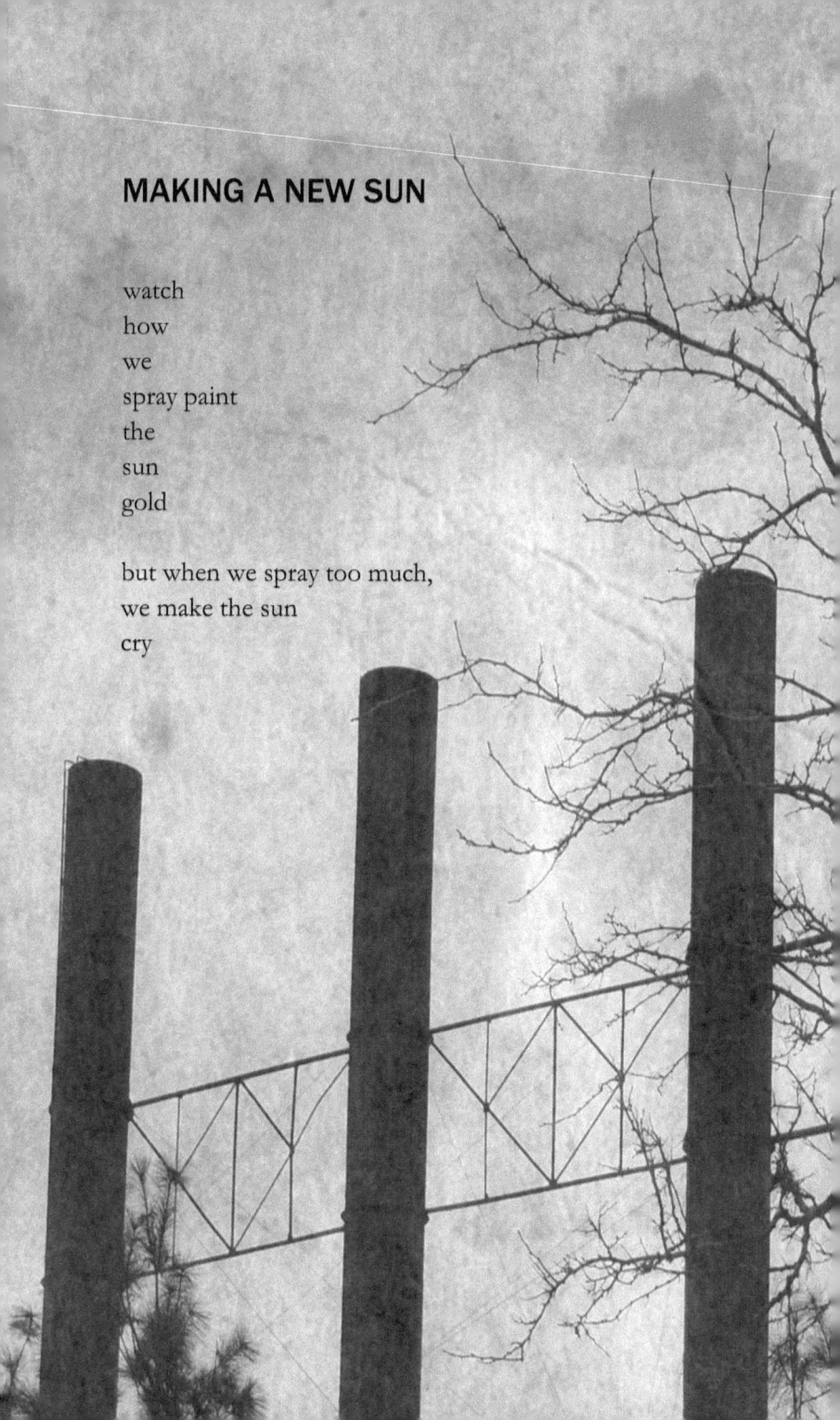

MAKING A NEW SUN

watch
how
we
spray paint
the
sun
gold

but when we spray too much,
we make the sun
cry

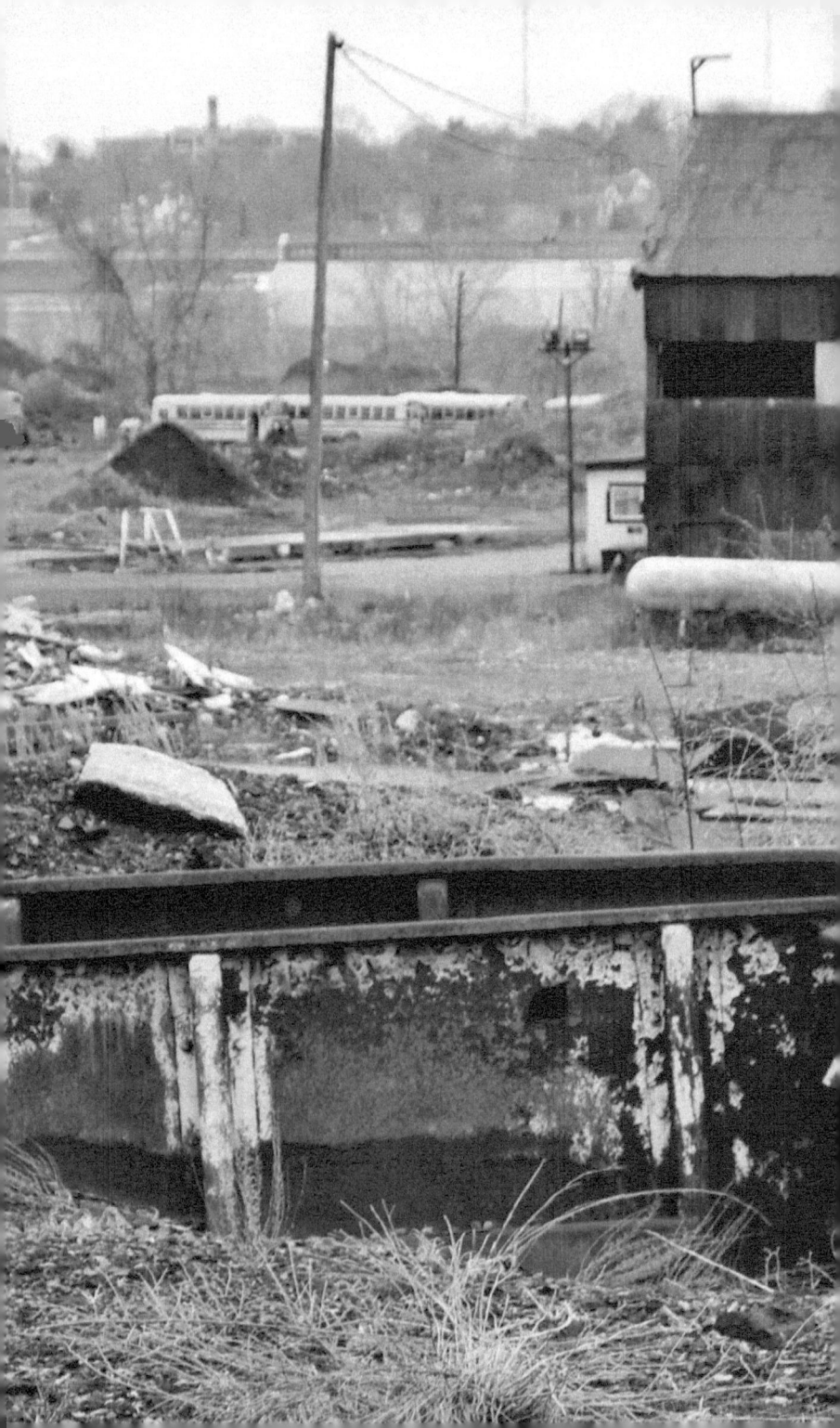

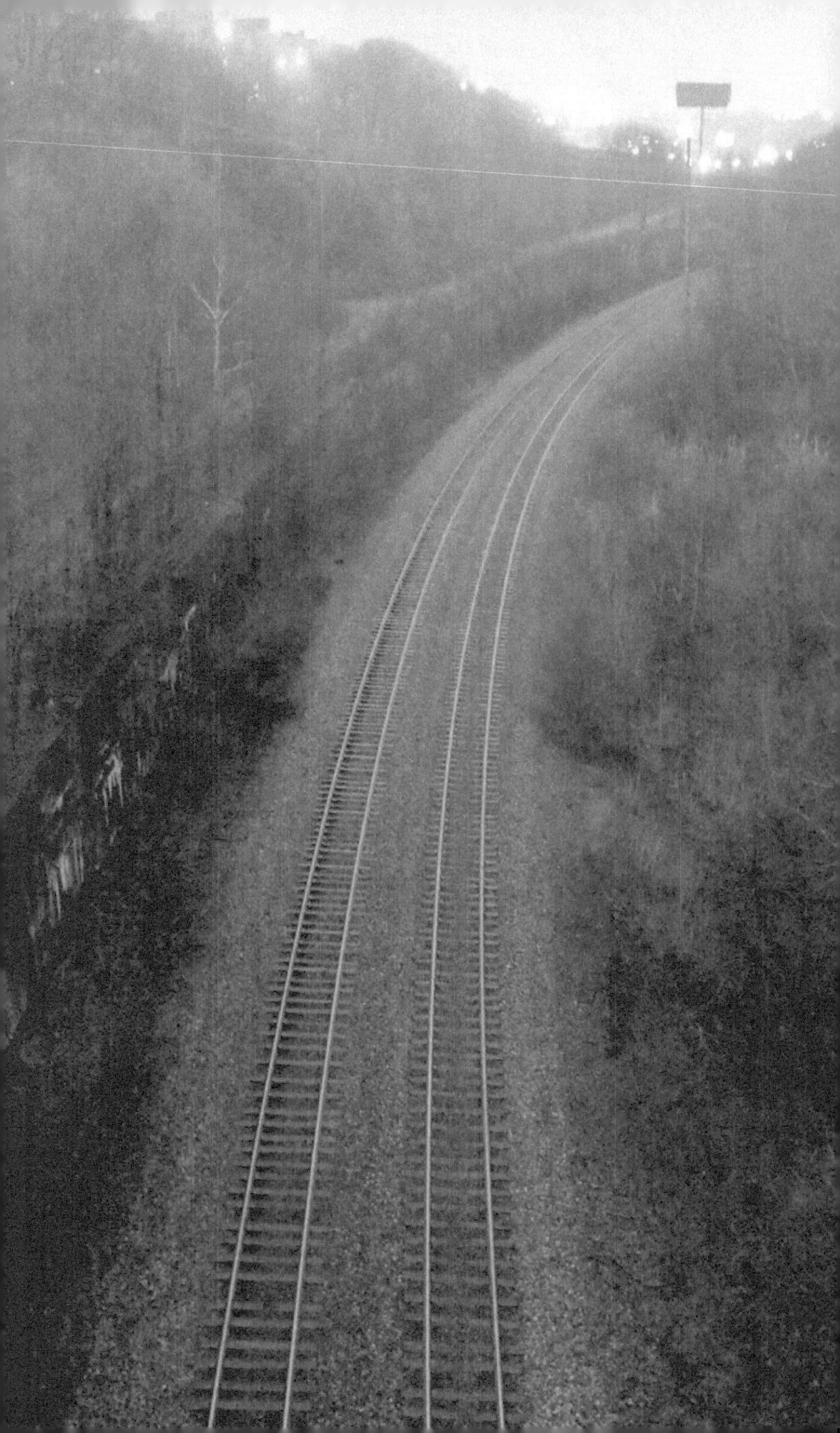

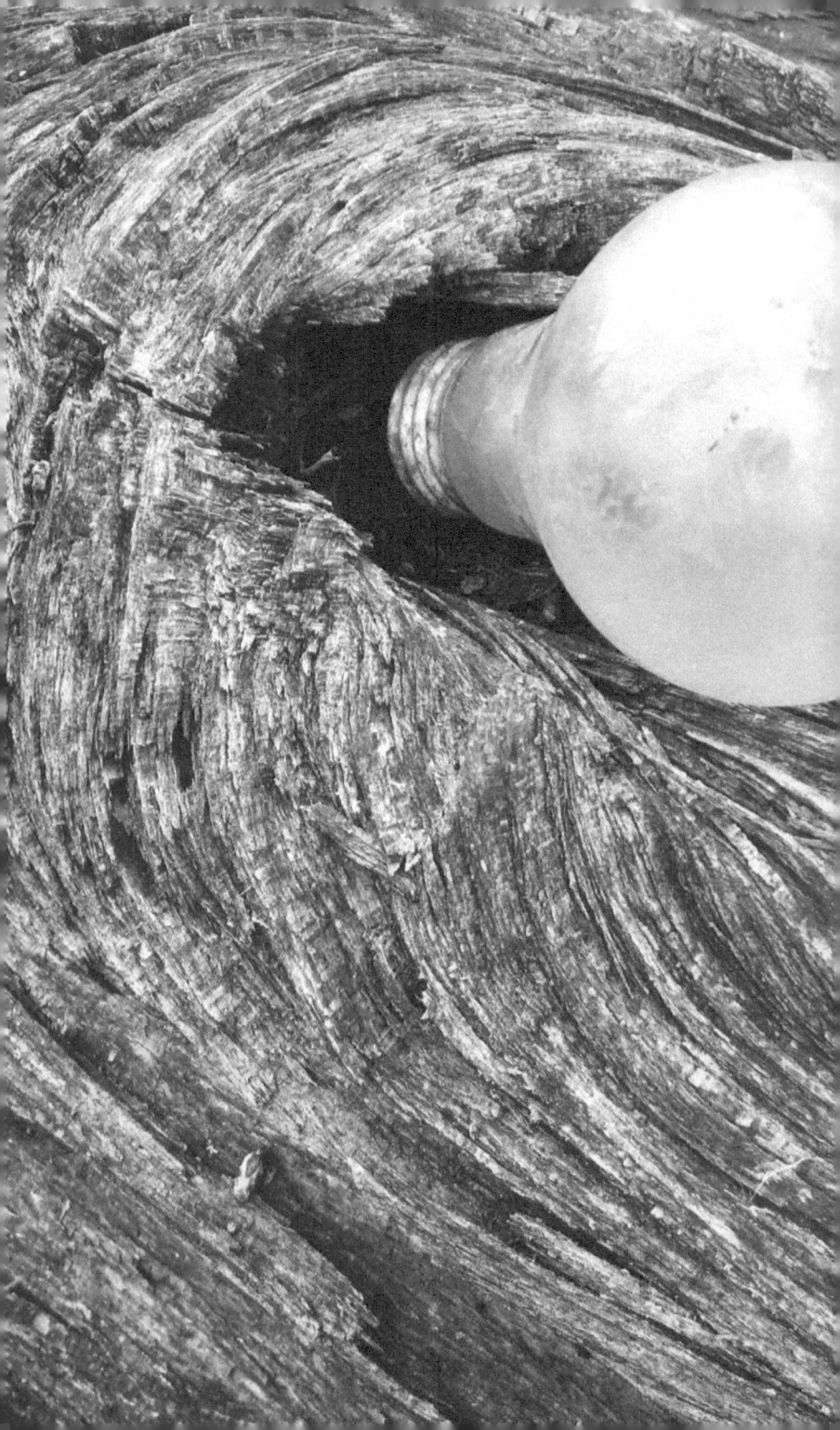

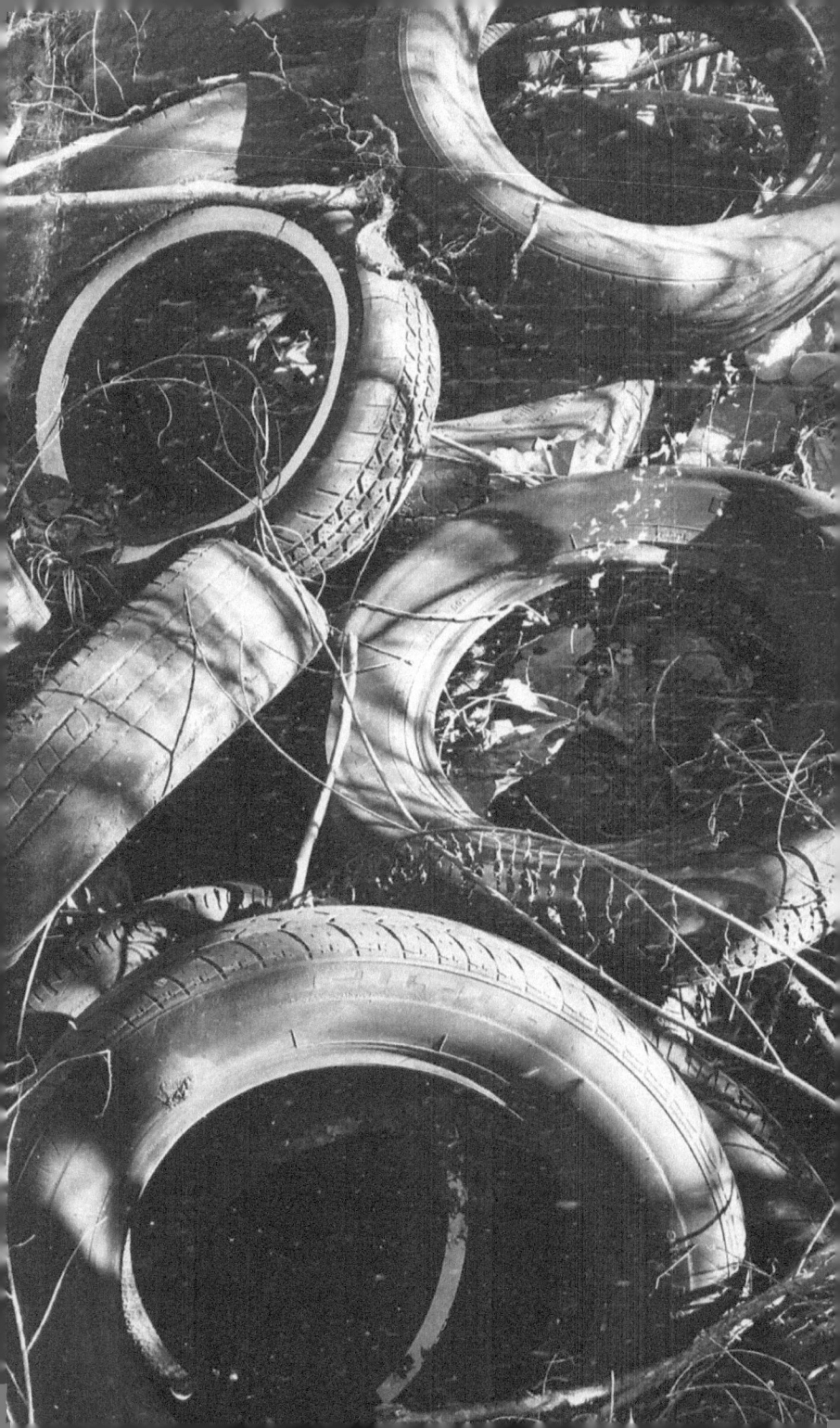

BELIEVELAND

Alas!
I found the alien portal
to the 4th Dimension
between the legs of
Olive Strange.

Don't know if
the Taco Bell parking lot
had anything to do with it—
because that's where we were, same as always but in a different spot.
And I don't know if
what I did will work for you
but don't count on it with her cos she's all mine now.

Anyway …

I've always been stuck in the 1st and 2nd Dimensions.
Her neon green ski mask never lifted
even while pulling off her shirt.
I'd salivate over her spicy taco meat-colored eyes, Cinnamon Twist-like hair, creamy youthful breasts slapping me in the face.
But my hands and eyes were only able to go from left to right, right to left,
up and down, down and up
(or make crazy zigzags and circles and trapezoids),

Then I found out giving her tokens lets me penetrate the 3rd Dimension.
She wants shiny gold token coins for a car wash since she's driving around a new Ford Explorer.
And the more tokens I give her, the longer I'm allowed between her legs to use my tongue, fingers, dick; her vibrator; etc.
The 3rd Dimension is glorious, but attainable by mostly anyone.

The precious 4th Dimension is no easy task.
It's been hidden from me because of the limitations of my perception.
It took time with her.
Time getting to know her—and her to know me.
Time getting to trust her—and her to trust me.
Time letting the past, present, and future all come together so I could see beyond her ski mask,
reach deep inside her head,
tickle her
beautiful
brain,
and give her
her gushing wet, screaming, record-breaking
167th multiple orgasm of the night.

Now I'm sitting in the passenger seat of Olive Strange's Explorer.
We just rode into and *through* a neon pink spray painted sunset headed deep into the unknown,
and speaking telepathically to y'all I'm like,
"Bye, bitches."

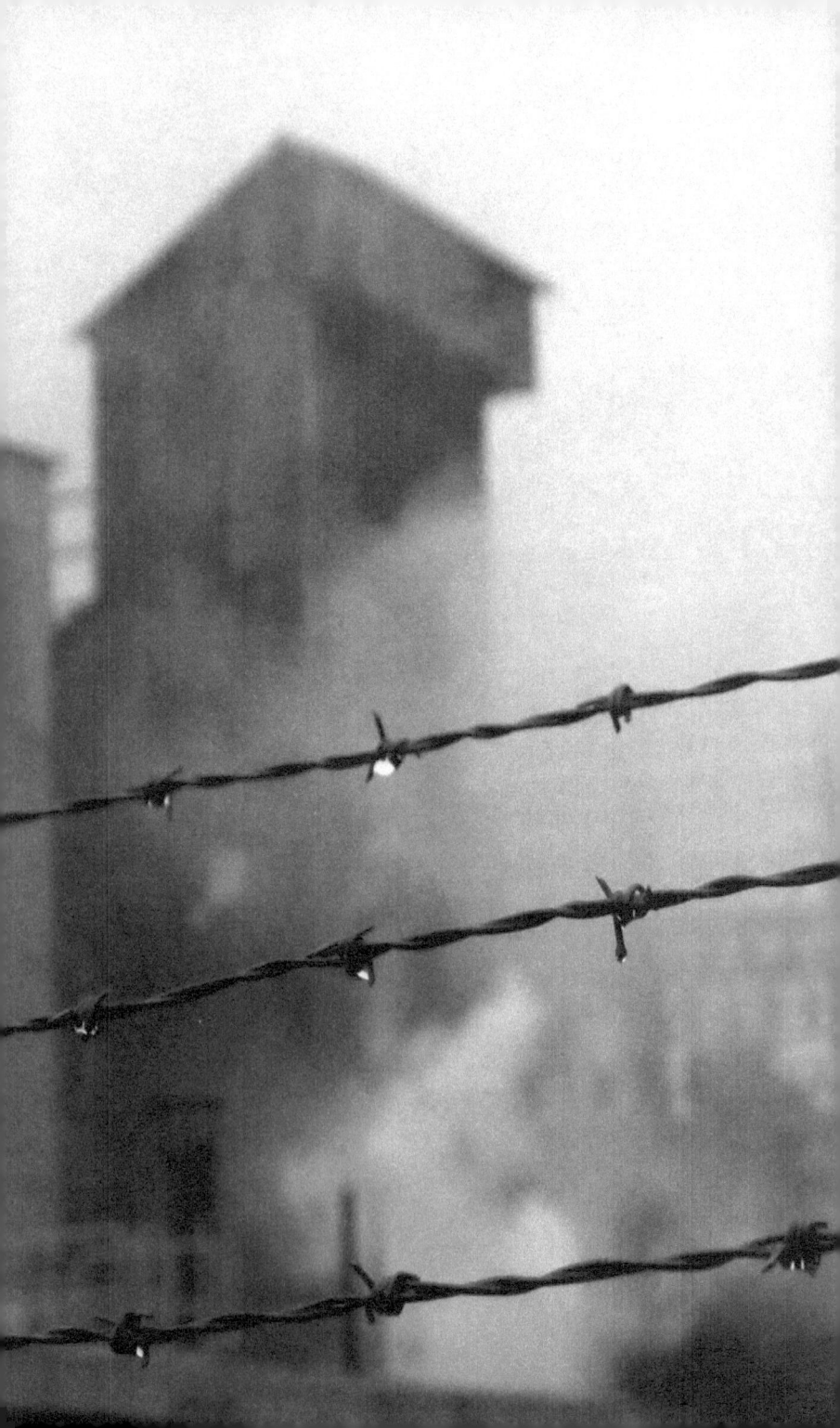

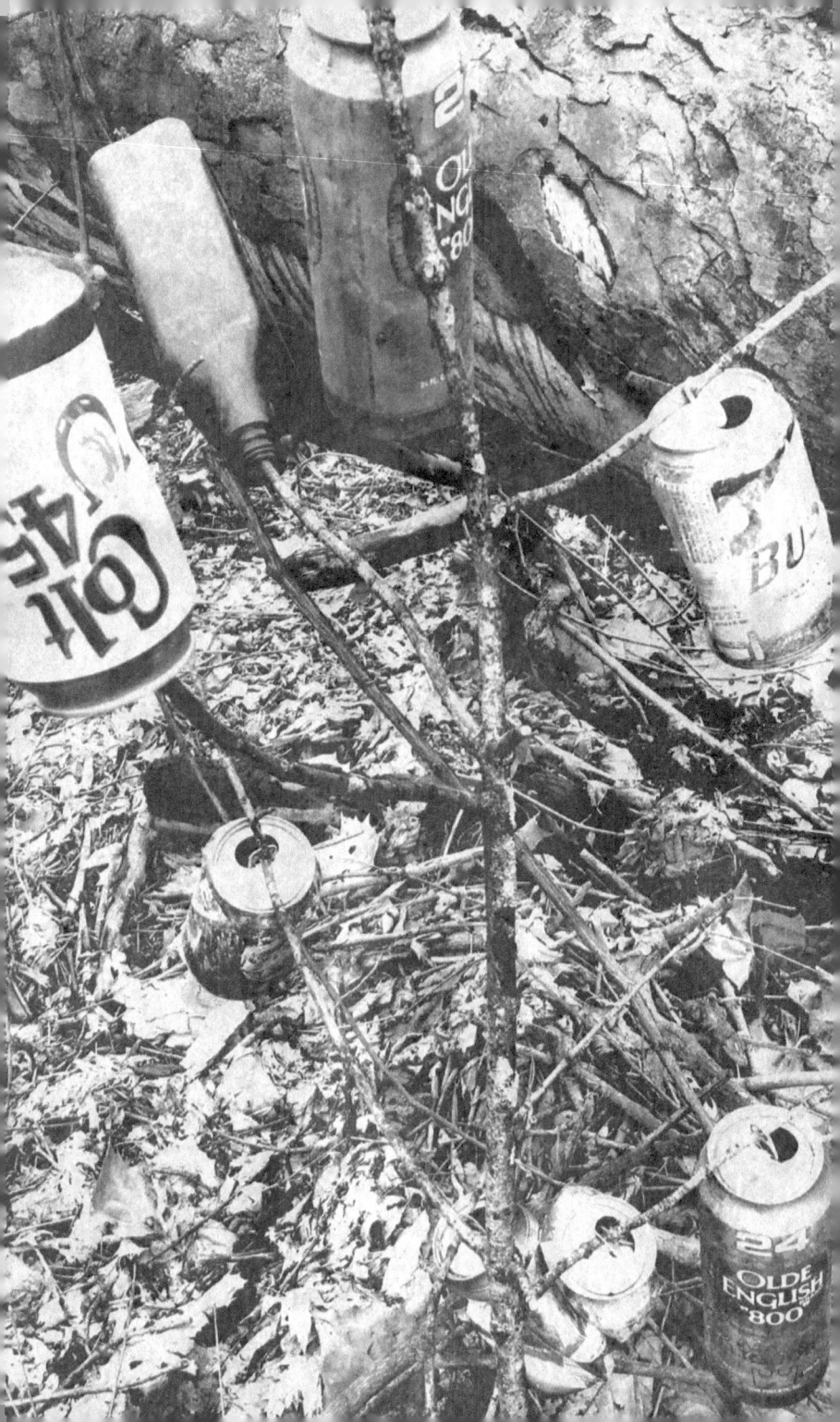

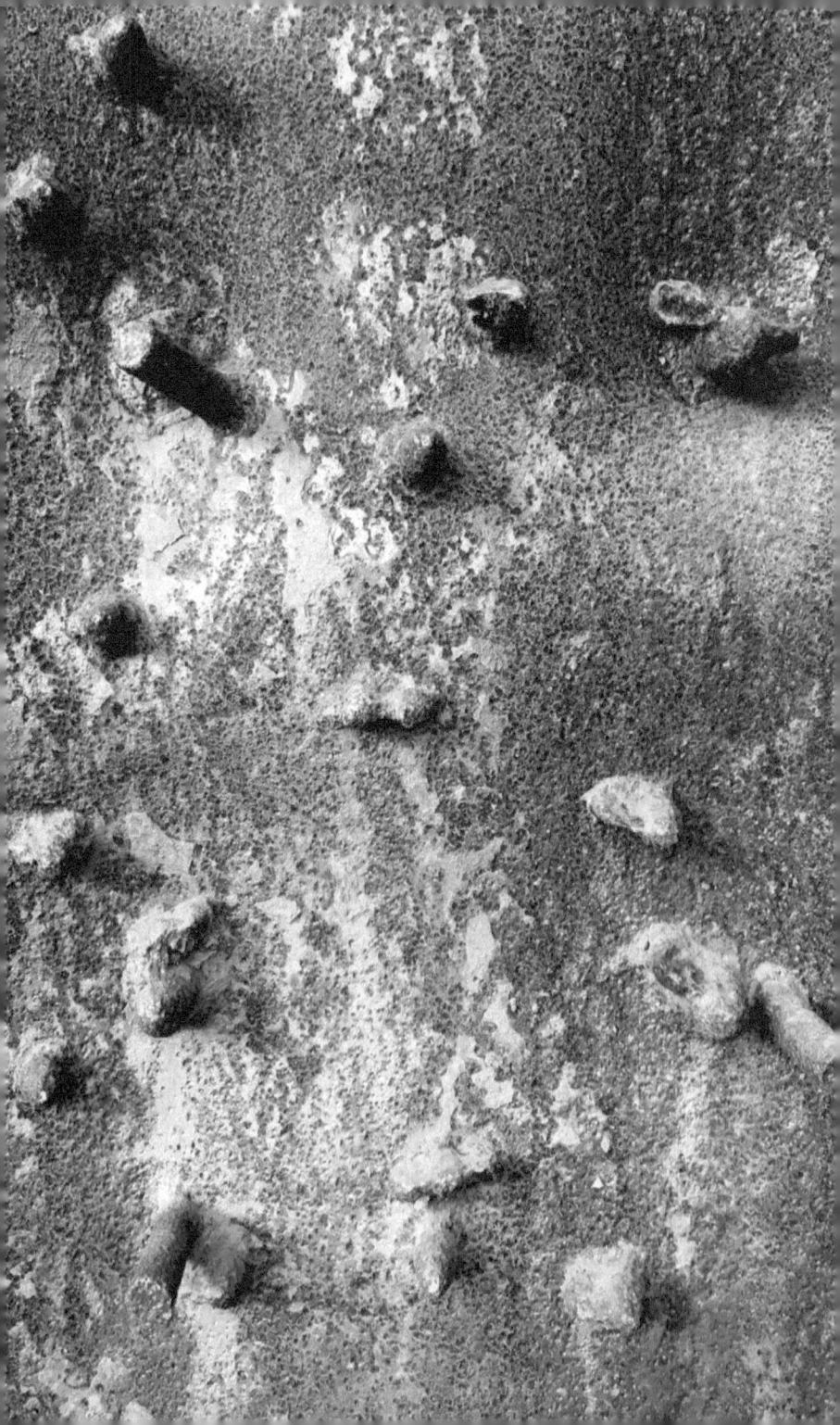

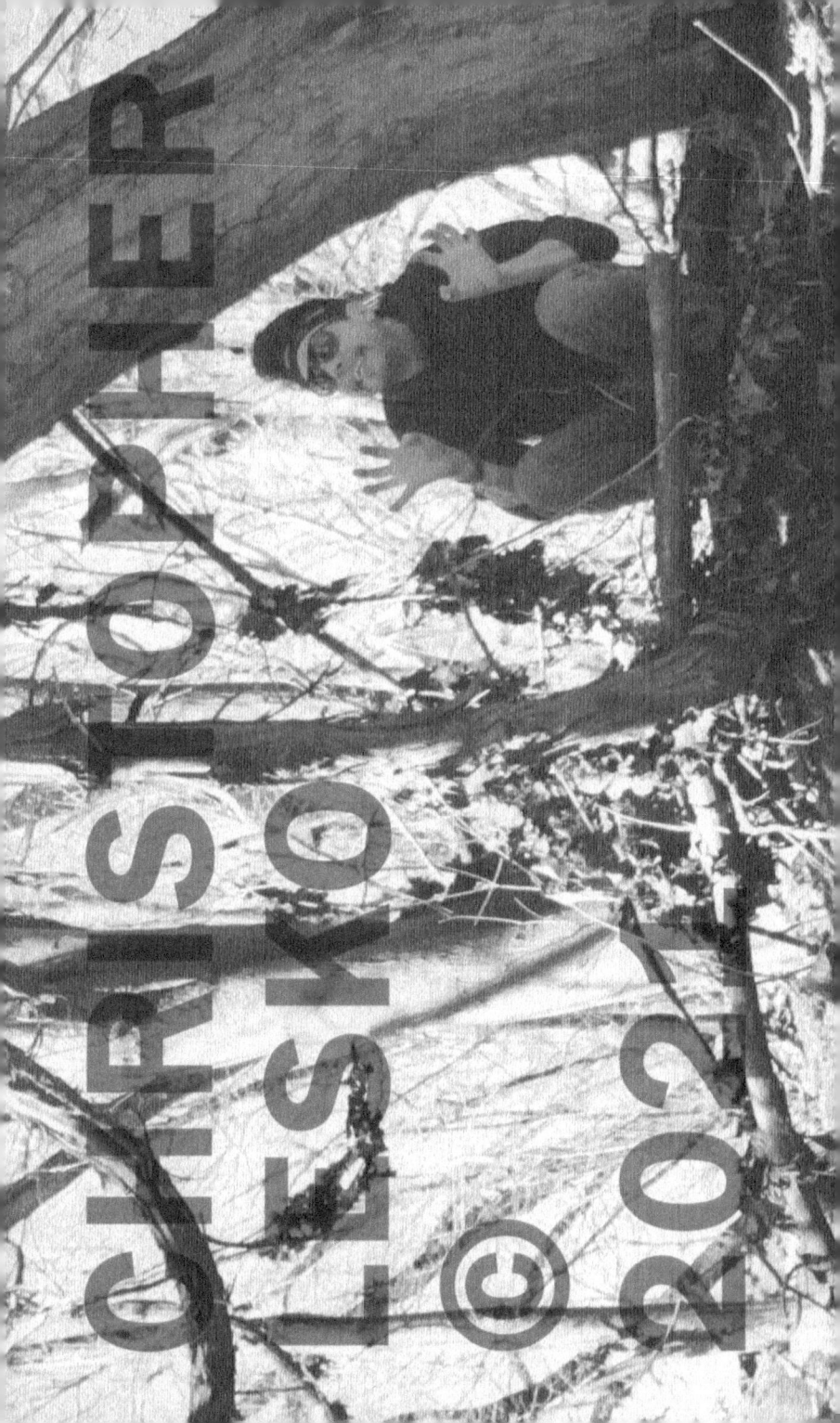

www.ingramcontent.com/pod-product-compliance
Lightning Source LLC
Chambersburg PA
CBHW030452220526
45464CB00006B/2510